CW01645112

DONKEY'S GLORY

Donkey's Glory

by

NAN GOODALL

with illustrations by

ADRIANA SAVIOZZI

MOWBRAY
LONDON & OXFORD

First published in 1944, nineteenth impression 1966
Second New Edition 1968, fourth impression 1975
Third New Edition, 1980
Reprinted 1987

This New Edition with Adriana Saviozzi illustrations (reproduced by permission of the Italian publishers, Nardini Editore) published 1980 by A.R. Mowbray & Co. Ltd, Saint Thomas House, Becket Street, Oxford, OX1 1SJ

ISBN 0264 66712 3 (*paper*)

Printed in Great Britain by
Billings Ltd., Worcester

DEDICATION

TO BISHOP KARNEY

TROTTEMENU

OFFERS HER HUMBLE OBEDIENCE

She woke up in the night and looked at him, sleeping in the moonlight

CONTENTS

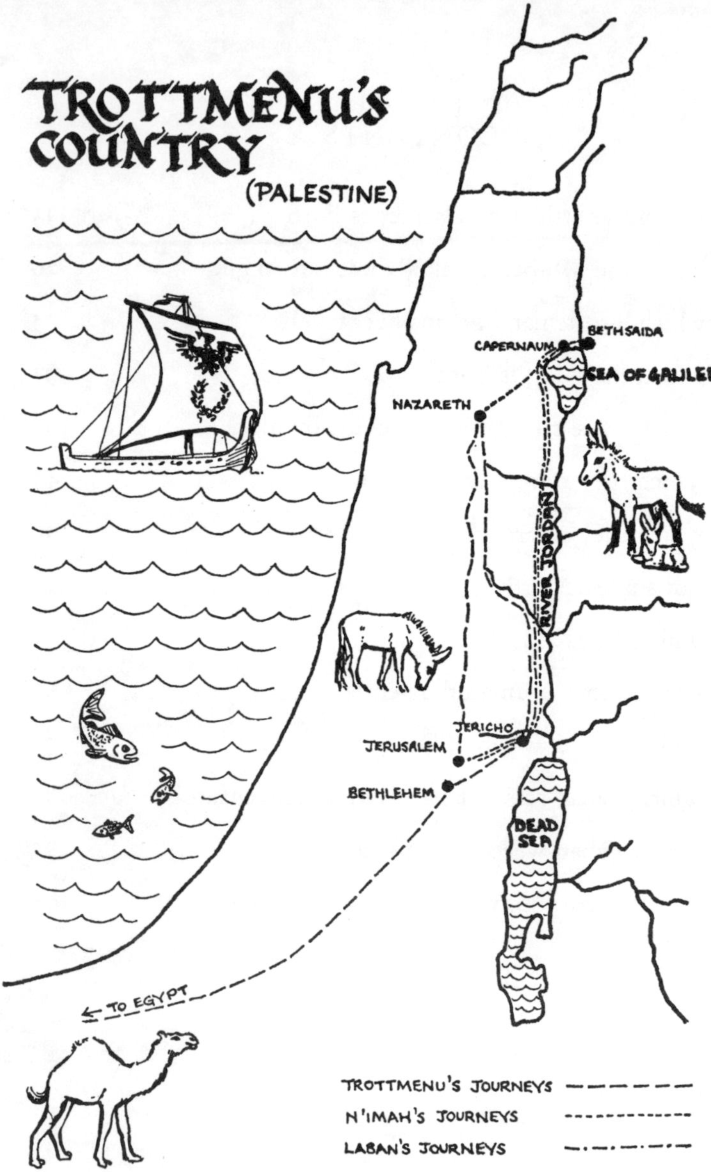

TROTTMENU'S COUNTRY
(PALESTINE)
BETHSAIDA
CAPERNAUM
SEA OF GALILEE
NAZARETH
RIVER JORDAN
JERICHO
JERUSALEM
BETHLEHEM
DEAD SEA
← TO EGYPT
TROTTMENU'S JOURNEYS
N'IMAH'S JOURNEYS
LABAN'S JOURNEYS

NAMES OF THE ANIMALS

TROTTEMENU, MÂCHELLANT	The traditional French mediaeval names of Ox and Ass. 'Fête de l'Âne' is still held at Beauvais.
SARI	Arab, meaning swift of foot.
ABU TAZAMMUR	Persian or Arabian, meaning Father of Scorn.
ABYAD	Persian, meaning white.
N'IMAH	Aramaic, meaning amiable.
JEMIMAH	Hebrew, meaning gentle as a dove.
TIRZAH	Hebrew, meaning pleasantness.
LABAN	Hebrew, meaning white.

O God,

Let me appear before You with these beasts
   Whom I so love because they bow their heads
Sweetly, and halting join their little feet
   So gently that it makes you pity them.

Francis Jammes.

CHAPTER ONE

In which the little grey Donkey is born

SHE WAS BORN in a small, square field right behind the village, and no one could have called her a pretty baby Donkey. She had a big head, and very thin legs with knobbly knees, and her shaggy little coat was neither grey nor brown at first. Just above the end of her nose she had a triangle of velvety-brown which she wrinkled up in a very comical manner when she was puzzled.

She began to run about almost as soon as she was born, round and round her Mother, and very often she tumbled over herself in her hurry, but her little legs quickly grew sturdy and strong. There was no hedge to the field, only heaps of stones to mark where it ended, so her Mother was fastened to the ground by a long rope, but she did not mind a bit because she was used to it; besides, it was quite long enough for her to nibble at such grass as there was.

One morning, very early, the little Donkey was just stretching and shaking herself after sleeping curled up all night, and opening her mouth very wide in a great yawn, when all at once she shut it again.

'Mother, who is this?' she asked.

There was a man walking across the field towards them. She pretended very hard that she was not frightened, but, all the same, she edged up close under her Mother's comfortable, warm grey coat.

'That is our Master,' said her Mother, and she gave a funny little soft cry of welcome.

The man looked quite kind, and he was smiling and holding

out his right hand. He came very close to them and from out of his hand came a most delicious smell which was quite new to the baby Donkey. Grass-smell she knew, which was cool and sweet, especially in the evening, and sand-smell she knew, which was hot and itchy and tickled her nose; but this smell she did not know. She peeped out from her hiding place and saw her Mother's velvety nose wrinkling up in the funny way that Donkey-noses have, before she gently put her lips right into the man's hand. Then she heard her Mother's big, sharp teeth crunching something.

'What is it?' she whispered.

'Ummmm!' said her Mother. 'Barley. Very good. Ummm!'

There was a sudden scuffle, a scurry of tiny hoofs, and the baby Donkey poked out her own nose, seized a handful of barley from the warm human hand, and was safely hidden again.

It was the best thing she had ever tasted, sweet and crunchy and with a toasty flavour. She poked her nose out again, but now the man was busy. He was fitting a rope of soft, plaited leather right over her Mother's nose and behind her ears, but he was not looking at all angry. In fact, he was smiling, and his hands felt quite friendly.

'Now you must go back to work,' he was saying. 'But I will not make you carry a very heavy load just yet, and your baby can come with you.'

He unfastened the rope, and led Mother-Donkey over the short grass.

'Oh, wait for me! Wait for me!' cried the baby Donkey. She would rather go anywhere than be left all alone.

'Walk behind me, then,' said her Mother, turning her head over her shoulder. 'And remember—do nothing to make our Master ashamed. I ought to have begun your lessons earlier, I suppose, but remember this—a good master is worth a sack full of barley, and he is only proud of a well-behaved Donkey.'

Away they went, stumbling a little over the loose stones and slithering a little on the grass because it was so dry, until they came to their Master's house.

It looked just like a small, square box, quite flat on the top, but it was so dazzlingly white against the blue sky that it seemed to sparkle like a house built of salt. Here Mother-Donkey was tied to a ring in the wall, and, presently, out came her Master's Wife. She was kind, too, and laughed at the shaggy little baby and tried to stroke her nose, but she backed away on her four obstinate little legs.

'I know,' said the Master's Wife, 'I know the very thing that you would like.'

She ran into the house and came out again with something so pretty that the little Donkey edged up close to see it better. It was such a lovely colour, pinky-orange, and smelt like the most delicious fruit in the world.

'Take it, silly!' said her Mother.

So she reached out her long neck and took it carefully with her soft little lips as she had seen her Mother do the barley.

It was even better than it looked, crisp and crackly and sweet and full of delicious juice that ran down her throat. And that was how she had her first carrot.

Her Mother was loaded up now, with two big baskets made of woven cords, red and yellow, hanging one on each side of her.

'Now go carefully,' said their Master, 'for this one has our best brown eggs in it, and some early figs that have just begun to turn red in the sun, and the other has tree-roots for firewood. Away we go!'

They all set off, the Master walking in front and his Wife following behind, leading the Donkey as well as carrying a great load on her back, for that was how they did things in that country; and trundling along last of all went an excited baby Donkey.

It was not very far into Nazareth, and it was not a very big town when they reached it. Donkeys were not allowed to walk down the main street with their loads, so they were tied up in a shady place. Their Master's Wife went a little distance away and unpacked all her wares and sat down on the pavement with them, together with a great many more farmers' wives. Some had live hens, some had heaps of vegetables, and some had firewood, too.

What a noise there was! The hens clucked and cackled, and one of them actually laid a big white egg on the pavement, and then stood there with her neck stretched out as if no hen had ever laid an egg before! There were crowds of people, too, all talking and shouting and laughing. There were boys playing on long pipes made of reeds, men playing drums, and men calling out what they had to sell.

One cried:

'Let me write your letters for you! I will do it while you wait. Let me write your letters for you!'

He carried his pen and ink all ready, and when he had written a letter he picked up a handful of sand and threw all over it to dry it.

Another cried:

'Who wants to drink? Come on, thirsty ones! Come and have a drink of water for nothing, without money!'

He did not really mean this, and when any one had drunk out of his leather bottle, he expected to be paid a penny.

There was such a coming and going, such a shouting and banging, that the little Donkey kept very close to her Mother, and soon they were at the end of a long row of Donkeys—grey Donkeys, brownish Donkeys, cream-coloured Donkeys, thin, half-starved Donkeys with sore backs where their loads rubbed, and fat, lazy Donkeys.

It grew dreadfully hot, and they were thirsty. Soon the little Donkey began to long for her field again. Flies kept settling on the middle of her back just where she could not reach them, and her eyes began to feel sore with the dust. Just when she was beginning to feel so miserable that she thought she could not bear it a minute longer, she heard her Master's voice, quite close. He was not speaking to her, but, all the same, her long furry ears cocked up in an inquisitive way.

'Peace be with you, Joseph Bar-Jacob,' she heard him say.

'And with you, peace,' came the answer.

'What a kind voice!' she thought, and pushed her nose out to look.

She saw standing quite near to her a tall man in a loose brown coat over a white tunic. She could really see his sandals better than anything, but she screwed and twisted her neck upwards until she could look between the legs of the Donkey nearest to her. She had not seen many human beings, but she thought this one was quite the nicest she had seen so far. He had such kind brown eyes, and he looked so happy, and his mouth was smiling above his dark beard.

'And what have you there?' asked her Master. 'Surely you are not selling anything? I thought you only made things.'

'I'm not exactly selling anything,' laughed Joseph. 'But I made this chest for Simon's daughter. She is getting married, and he promised to fetch it away for her; but he hasn't turned up and I can't find him anywhere.'

'It's a good chest. Well-polished, and well made, too.'

'Yes. I certainly put some of my best work into it.'

'It is a beautiful chest. Suppose Simon doesn't come for it?'

'Then I shall have to take it home again.'

'I suppose . . . I suppose you wouldn't like to sell it to me, would you, Joseph?'

'But why should you want a chest? You have no daughters.'

'No, but it would please my wife. I have taken a fancy for it. Come, how much will you take for it?'

'But perhaps Simon will come for it next week.'

'You can make him another.'

Joseph laughed again.

'The chest is not for sale,' he said. 'And, if it were, you would not want to carry it all the way to your farm.'

'I could put it on my Donkey over there.'

Joseph turned, still smiling, to look, and somehow or other, his eye caught the comical grey face with the brown velvet triangle above the nose that was just sticking out from the long, neat line of Donkeys.

'Inquisitive listeners have long ears!' he said.

Soon he was standing very close to her, gently brushing the flies from her coat. His long, firm fingers found, too, the secret tickly-spot just behind her ears, and rubbed it so comfortably that the little Donkey closed her eyes with pleasure.

'I'll give her to you for the chest,' said her Master, suddenly.

'But I don't want a Donkey,' protested Joseph.

'Some day you may. You could make her carry wood for your carpenter's shop.'

'She's too small.'

'She will grow.'

'I'll tell you what, Reuben—if you want the chest so much, you shall have it. But keep your little donkey for the present, and, if I want her, I will fetch her before a year is up.'

'Done!' cried Reuden, joyfully, and immediately set to work to fasten the chest onto Mother-Donkey's back with thin cords.

It was quite cool when they set off for home, and they trotted along happily. The chest was not heavy, and, fortunately, their Master's Wife had been able to sell everything that she had brought. How good and cool their field smelt to their noses when at last they were back, and how fresh the grass seemed to their hot and dusty little hoofs! The little grey Donkey was so excited by all that she had seen and heard that she chattered away softly to her Mother until the sky turned dark blue with night and the silver points of the stars began to appear.

CHAPTER TWO

In which the Mother-Donkey meets an Angel

VERY SOON every one in the Market Place knew her and loved her. She trotted so merrily behind her Mother that her tiny, polished hoofs twinkled like sunbeams.

'Tick-tack, tick-tack,' she went over the stones, and 'Ticker-tacker, ticker-tacker,' when she went faster; and sometimes when they were in a great hurry and she had to run to keep up, her hoofs went 'ticketty-tacketty ticketty-tacketty, tack, tack.'

All the little boys would run out when they heard her coming, and soon they had a name for her, a name that sounded exactly like the noise she made. She was called TROTTEMENU.

When she was alone with her Mother, tied up against the house wall or in the field, she had to learn her lessons.

'Now say after me,' her Mother would begin, 'the Two Great Donkey Rules:

I must never lift the hoof to kick,
I must never bare the tooth to bite.'

And Trottemenu would repeat the Donkey Rules very solemnly after her Mother, and promise to keep them. She had to learn, too, the Donkey Promise.

'I promise my Owner,' she recited, 'these things:

Whither thou goest, I go too,
Whatsoever thou sayest, I will do,
I will serve thee faithfully,
Obey thee cheerfully,
As long as I stand on my four hoofs.'

Then there was a whole list of Rules For Good Manners to learn, such as, 'I must keep my nose from Snatching and Tasting.'

'But, Mother,' she said, 'suppose I saw just one very little carrot that some one had dropped and forgotten in the Market Place? Couldn't I pick that up?'

'Not so much as one little carrot,' said her Mother, firmly. 'You may only take what is offered to you on the hand.'

So she grew wiser and wiser every day, and soon she was able to carry small bundles herself, especially the firewood, because she could not break that. Sometimes she met Joseph in the Market Place, and he always came over to her and stroked her, and she liked this very much and rubbed her head against his coat, in a pleased way.

One day, in her first summer, it was very hot and she and her Mother were standing in their field and wondering if their Master would want them to go out to work. Trottemenu felt sleepy and blinked at the grass lazily. Suddenly something that seemed to her very strange happened. A little, cool wind ruffled all up her coat, and the grass, which before was hot and scorched, instantly turned fresh and bright green and smelt as if it had just rained.

She looked up at the sky, and there, against the blue, she saw something white. It was only a flash, something like a sea-gull flying above the sea in the sunlight. Yet it seemed to come nearer. Then she did not quite know what did happen. Between her and her Mother was a pair of great, shining wings, neither white nor silver, but both at once. She thought, too, she had a glimpse of golden hair above a lovely face. Then, like magic, it was gone again, and they were quite alone in their hot field.

Before she could speak, her Mother turned to her, and said, in a very serious voice,

'Trottemenu, I have had a Vision.'

At this Trottemenu looked very excited, although, to tell the truth, she had not any idea at all what a Vision was. She thought that perhaps it was a very special kind of carrot.

'Did it taste good?' she asked, innocently.

'You are a very silly little Donkey,' said her Mother, crossly.

'I'm sorry, Mother,' she said, and hung her head so humbly that her Mother instantly forgave her.

'I have seen and heard A Very Strange Thing', went on her Mother.

'Well,' said Trottemenu, eagerly, 'I, too, thought I saw some one all shining silver and white and gold.'

'I think it was an Angel,' said her Mother, solemnly. 'There was a voice in my ear like the wind, yet not the wind, like big trees rustling their leaves, yet not trees. It said this to me:

"The Little Grey Donkey shall be a King's playfellow,
And her Daughter shall see wonderful things;
But the Snow-white Donkey shall carry the King in his Triumph
And everybody shall laugh and sing." '

'What does it mean?' asked Trottemenu, wondering.

'I don't know,' admitted her Mother, 'but, without a doubt it is very important, and you must never forget it.'

So they stood close together and recited it over and over again until they had it by heart.

When the spring came round again, Joseph came to fetch Trottemenu away. She wished her Mother good-bye and promised to be good, and went away very proudly, feeling quite grown-up to have a Master of her own.

Joseph lived at the other end of Nazareth, in a tiny, square, white house, and in the wall was a brand-new ring for Trottemenu to be tied to. It was a good place to stand because there was a fig-tree against the house wall to shade her from the sun in summer. The fig-leaves were just uncurling like five little green fingers, and at first she was very tempted to nibble at them, but then she remembered her lessons on manners.

She thought a great deal about the Angel's words, but she did not see how they could be true. Joseph, however kind he was, could not possibly be a king, because he was a carpenter, and the only other person that Trottemenu knew was Mary.

She loved Mary from the very first minute that she set eyes on her, in the house straight opposite Joseph's. She loved her gentle, beautiful face and her kind eyes, and her shining brown hair, and even her blue dress. One day, very soon, Joseph was going to marry Mary, and he had told Trottemenu this one night as a great secret. She was very glad that her dear Joseph should have a wife like Mary, and she spent a long time every day thinking out what she could do to please them.

Soon she had to learn to wear a bridle and to have a little metal bit in her mouth. At first she did not like it at all, and it made the corners of her soft, velvety lips so sore that she could not eat the armful of grass that Joseph cut for her. Then Mary cooked a special potful of beans all for her, and mashed them up and brought them to her, soft and warm and comforting to her poor mouth, and, after a few days, she did not even notice her bit. She had a little saddle, too, of yellow leather, but this was a specially soft one, made by Joseph himself, so that she never had a rubbed back, such as she saw on other Donkeys.

She had not been there very long before a second strange thing happened to her. She was standing under her fig-tree, feeling very contented. The sunlight was warm but not too hot on her back, and everything was very quiet. She could look through the little square window opposite, which was really just a hole cut in the house wall, and see Mary inside. Mary was sitting on a stool, in her blue dress, and doing some very beautiful embroidery. It was a pattern of orange-branches on cream linen, and it looked so real that Trottemenu could almost smell the scented white petals of the orange-flowers and the round golden fruit as the needle went in and out. Mary was singing softly as she worked.

Then, from nowhere at all, a little wind crept out, and once again Trottemenu's grey coat ruffled all up. At the same time, she seemed to smell and see everything at once that she thought most beautiful—long grass with the dew on it, a whole field of rippling barley, trees with big, shady green leaves. Yet all the while she was still looking in at the window.

Who was that, standing by Mary? There were the glittering wings, the gleam of golden hair and the half-seen, beautiful face. Even while she looked, it seemed to grow misty and faint and melt away, and she was staring in at Mary, all alone. But Mary was kneeling down now, by her stool, her hands together, and the embroidery lay forgotten on the floor.

Trottemenu stood quite quiet and still. Presently, Mary came out to her, and put her arms round her neck and kissed her furry head between the ears.

'My darling little Trottemenu,' she whispered. 'God is sending me a very wonderful gift. I shall have a little Son, and He will be a King.'

Then Trottemenu took a step or two away, and she bent her knobbly front knees and lowered her head, and made a most beautiful curtsey to Mary.

CHAPTER THREE

In which Trottemenu begins her travels

THEY WERE GOING on a journey. Trottemenu stood outside the little white house, and Joseph kept running in and out carrying things they were to take. He brought two yellow rush mats which were to be beds for Mary and himself, and two big scarlet and orange rugs in case they should be cold at night. These he rolled up very tightly into bundles and hung on her back. Then he hung over her shoulders some cloth bags that Mary had stitched, and in one were dates and raisins for them to eat on the way, in another some flat, hard bread like biscuit and a little pot of honey, and in the third were beans and barley for Trottemenu herself, for they never forgot her. She wondered where they could possibly be going, so far away that they had to take sleeping rugs and things to eat. She knew that it would be dark early, for it was winter, but, even so, they must be leaving Nazareth far behind.

When she was loaded up, Joseph came to her and fixed her little yellow saddle on her back, above all the odd-shaped rolls and bundles.

'Now, Trottemenu,' he said, stroking her neck, 'we have to go a very long way. Every one in the land has orders to go to the village where they really belong, so that the people can all be counted up. We shall have to go all the way to Bethlehem, for that is really my home-town.'

She rubbed her head against him to show that she was ready to go, although she did wonder what was going to happen to Mary while they were away.

Soon she had a great surprise. Mary herself came out, and

Joseph put his arm round her and tucked her all up in a big grey cloak and lifted her up onto Trottemenu's back.

'I shall have to go very carefully,' she thought, but she was really glad that Mary was coming with them.

'Away!' cried Joseph, and clicked his tongue to show that they were ready, so off they set.

Trottemenu's bundles bumped and bounced against her shaggy little sides, the beans and barley rattled, and, going downhill, Mary had to hold on very hard so that she would not slide right over Trottemenu's head. However, when they came to the worst bits, there was Joseph walking along by their side, his right arm round Mary, to hold her on, and in his left hand a big stick, in case they met any robbers.

Soon they were on a good main road, and she trotted along quite happily. All through the day her little hoofs went, but they began to get rather slow towards dark. When it grew too dark to see along the road, Joseph would very carefully help Mary down. They would stretch themselves, then they would look round for shelter. There were all kinds of little enclosed yards along the roads, built for Horses and Donkeys. They had four walls all round, except for a little opening to go in by, and no roof, but Joseph and Mary did not mind this at all, because they liked to lie and watch the stars. They would unroll their mats and their rugs and sit on them to eat their bread and honey and dates, and Trottemenu would stand close to them, chewing a handful of beans and barley.

'What is that terrible noise?' asked Joseph once, looking quite alarmed. But Mary laughed.

'It's only Trottemenu crunching dry beans,' she said.

Joseph always remembered to take her down to the river before they went to bed. That was great fun. She would pick her way delicately over the loose stones until she came to water just deep enough to cover her wrinkled-up nose. Then she would suck and suck and suck, great cold gulps of water, and feel, at the same time, her hoofs sinking into a delicious cool squelch of mud.

All night she stood by them, without her saddle and bridle, while they slept, and if she heard the slighest noise she lifted

up her head and blinked sleepily, in case it was robbers.

The third day seemed even longer, and they were all rather tired. There were a great many people on the road, too, all going to be counted. They hardly noticed how pretty it was as they passed through Jericho, with palm-groves and flower-gardens that would smell beautiful in summer, and walls and palaces. It was quite dark when at last they came into Bethlehem, and Trottemenu stumbled wearily along. To make it worse, the streets were crowded, every one pushing and shouting and running about. She could hardly make her way through the people, and, when she tried to get past, some of them hit her over the nose or jerked at her bridle so that it hurt her mouth.

At last they worked their way as far as the Khan they were looking for, the inn where travellers could put up for the night. The courtyard seemed very full. Camels were kneeling down all over the place. Donkeys and Mules tied up against all the walls, boys running about offering to unpack luggage in return for pennies, and servants threading their way among it all with trays of food.

'It seems very crowded,' said Joseph, doubtfully. 'Perhaps I'd better find the innkeeper himself. Don't move away from here, Trottemenu.'

He left them in a corner near the gate, and soon he came back with the innkeeper. He was a fat, jolly, red-faced man in an orange tunic, a red sash, and a purple turban; but Joseph was looking very worried and unhappy.

As soon as he saw them again, he called out,

'He says there is no room for us.'

'No room at all,' said the innkeeper. 'I have every room quite full and even people sleeping on the roof.' And he laughed as if he did not mind at all.

'But we've been travelling for three days,' said Joseph.

'Some people have been on the road for more than a week,' said the innkeeper.

'Then we shall have to go on and see if we can find somewhere outside the town, not too far away.'

He looked at Mary, and she was looking so pale and tired that he thought he could hardly bear it.

'I'll tell you what . . .' said the innkeeper, thoughtfully, watching them look at each other, 'but you wouldn't like it . . .'

'What is it?' asked Joseph, eagerly, anxious only to find somewhere for Mary to rest.

'Well, there's a little place just across the courtyard, where we sometimes put horses and oxen. It's not bad. It's quite clean and comfortable.'

Joseph made up his mind at once.

'We'll take it,' he said.

The innkeeper was not really at all a bad fellow, so he led them right across the courtyard himself, and, just outside, they came to a kind of cave in the wall.

'There you are, then!' he said. 'I'll send a boy with a lamp in a minute.'

It was very dark inside when they peered in, but the innkeeper kept his promise, and soon a curly-headed little boy in a short, green tunic came running along with a lamp, in such a hurry that he nearly spilt all the oil out of it, but Mary thanked him with a lovely smile.

'Why, it's splendid!' cried Joseph, going in first and holding the lamp up. 'It's quite dry and comfortable, and we shall be all alone and quiet.'

He helped Mary down and took her into the cave.

'It has two separate halves!' she cried in delight. 'Look! Up this step is another part! I know what we could do. We could have the top half and Trottemenu could have the lower half all to herself. She would like that.'

It did not take very long for them to get settled in. They put their rugs and mats down on the floor and stood the lamp far enough away to be safe. What queer, flickering shadows it threw on the walls! And shadows like big, black birds danced all over the stone roof. Joseph found some long planks of wood leaning against one side of the cave, and, after a good deal of pulling and tugging, he managed to fix up a kind of barrier between their half and Trottemenu's half, so that it was just exactly like home, with Mary and Joseph safe and snug inside their own house.

Trottemenu could not see them, but she could hear them talking softly and sleepily. It was very dark on her side of the barrier. Her saddle and bridle were hanging over the top of it, where Joseph had carefully put them, and she was quite free, so she decided to do a little exploring for herself before she went to bed.

First of all, she gave herself a good shake to shake all the dust out of her coat, then she snorted very softly down her nose to get the dust out of that, then she flicked her ears very quickly backwards and forwards. Then she set out to explore.

It felt like straw, up in that very dark corner. She could hear it rustling under her hoofs. She scraped at it delicately with one foot. Yes, it was straw. She would make herself a little bed in that corner.

But what was happening? The whole wall of the cave was gradually heaving out and coming at her. The floor was rising up in a great, brown bump. Some one was breathing, close to her. Trottemenu's heart turned over with fear. The biggest animal she had ever seen was gradually rising to its feet in that very dark corner and standing over her.

Poor Trottemenu! She longed for Joseph, but she knew that he was safely asleep by now, on the other side of the barrier.

'Who are you?' she managed to quaver, in a thin little voice.

'It's who are YOU, I should think!' answered a voice so low and deep that it seemed to rumble all along the floor. 'This is my usual bed-place.'

'I'm very sorry,' said Trottemenu, humbly. 'We are travellers, and we haven't anywhere else to go.'

'Why didn't you say so before?' grumbled the voice.

She wanted to say that she had not had very much chance, but she did not think it would be very polite. Instead, she said:

'I am Trottemenu, the Donkey of Mary and Joseph.'

She said it very proudly, with her head tossed back, standing there in the dark.

'And I'm Mâchellant,' came the answer. 'Mâchellant the Ox, and I'm coming out to look at you.'

He lumbered out, and stood just where Joseph's lamp threw a little pool of light over the barrier.

He was not so very frightening after all, in spite of his size. He had a great, big head, with two long, curving horns, but his eyes were brown and very kind. He wore a coat of short, shining, reddish-brown hair.

'Are you happy?' he asked, unexpectedly.

'Yes, very happy,' she said. 'Aren't you?'

'Oxen are never happy,' he answered. 'We go round and round, up and down, round and round, treading corn and dragging the plough, and if we get tired they stick a sharp spike into us. They've done that to my family for thousands of years now.'

Trottemenu's soft little heart was touched, and she snuggled against Mâchellant in a very friendly way. They talked in whispers for a while, about all the things they had seen in their lives, then Trottemenu's voice gradually grew fainter and fainter, and she fell asleep, warm and comfortable against Mâchellant's brown coat.

CHAPTER FOUR

In which the King is born

THEY WERE STILL THERE the next day, and the khan was more crowded than ever. People kept pouring in and being told there was no room, and standing and arguing about it. You couldn't even walk across the yard for camels and bundles and people camping out. Joseph went out once to see if he could find somewhere to stay, but he came back so tired that Mary said they were very happy where they were.

It was beautifully quiet all by themselves, and Joseph only laughed when he found Mâchellant sharing their lodgings. The little, curly boy in green brought out some wine for Mary, and some fresh raisins, and even a little silver fish cooked in milk. He came to feed Mâchellant, too, with a great armful of hay, and Trottemenu shared it with him. At night they lit their lamp, just as before, and listened to all the noises of the khan in the distance.

Trottemenu did not know what made her wake up with a start. She did not know how long she had been asleep. She listened, but there was not a sound. They were all asleep in the courtyard; Mary and Joseph were quite silent, and Mâchellant was asleep; yet she knew that something had happened.

She went quietly to the door and looked out. Not a sound. She looked up at the sky. It was like dark blue velvet, but just above her head a single star burnt like a silver cross against the blue. Then she heard the singing.

It sounded as if it came from out on the hills. She could only just hear it faintly on the wind, but it was the loveliest sound she

had ever heard, thousands and thousands of voices, singing just like birds. There was suddenly a little puff of wind, and she thought she could hear quite distinctly,

'Glory to God in the Highest.'

Then it all faded again. She stared at the sky in the distance, straining her eyes, and it was not blue, but gold. Then she saw that it was a cloud of angels, bearing up and up and up with great golden wings, singing like birds as they went, until they came to the golden gates of Heaven and all went inside.

She stood perfectly still, all alone in the cool night, thinking. She glanced up. Yes, the one silver star was still there, above her head. She wondered what it all meant. She stood there a very long time, her head bent in thought.

There was a noise up the street. Some one was running. Some one was running right down the street in the middle of the night. Some one else was running behind. Now there were three. Now they were nearly here. You could hear them panting. They were turning in at the courtyard entrance, running right between the sleepers, jumping over the bundles of rugs. Trottemenu remembered too late that she had meant to guard the cave. She tried to turn, but a boy runner pushed past her before she could stop him. Two men in sheepskin coats followed, almost sobbing for breath, hardly able to stand. Straight up to the barrier they went, and pulled the planks away and made a hole. Then they all three crowded together and looked through, and, as soon as they had looked, they went down on their knees.

Presently they rose, and went out very quietly, on tip-toe, but as soon as they were in the courtyard they began to dance and jump about and sing and shout.

'It's true! It's true!' they shouted. 'Just as the Angel said out on the hills!'

Every one began to wake up, grumbling and stretching and yawning, and the camels fidgeted and coughed like cross old men, and people all began asking questions, while the two men and the boy ran about all over the place, telling people how they had been minding sheep when an Angel had come and told them to run as quickly as they could to Bethlehem.

Trottemenu was very worried by all the noise, and she hoped that Joseph and Mary were safe and not being frightened. She went softly over to the hole in the boards that the shepherds had made, and peeped through.

'Mâchellant! Mâchellant!' she began to call, in a very excited voice, and he could tell at once that something very extraordinary had happened.

He lumbered over to her, and together they each put an eye to the hole.

There, not a yard away from them, all lit up and turned to gold by the lamp, were Joseph and Mary, and between them, in an old wooden manger, lay a tiny, new-born Baby, sound asleep.

Trottemenu took a last look, then she gently went down on her knobbly knees. Mâchellant looked at her rather shyly for a minute, then he, too, went down onto the great round pads that were his knee-caps, and so they knelt quietly side by side, their heads bent down.

CHAPTER FIVE

In which three strange Riders come by night

THREE FIGURES were hunched against the sky, wrapped in their cloaks. They stood, quite still and silent, looking down on Bethlehem. Were they robbers? Trottemenu shivered.

She stood in her little yard and felt frightened. After three days the crowd had all gone away from the khan, all the travellers and all the camels.

'What shall we do?' asked Mary. 'The Baby Jesus is too tiny to travel all that way home. He would be cold.'

'We will find a little house in Bethlehem,' said Joseph, 'and stay here for a while.'

So Joseph found a tiny white house, a square one, and soon they were settled in there. Mary wrapped the Baby Jesus up in long bands of linen, right from just under his arms down to his toes, and they carried him very carefully to their new house and there they stayed for over a year. It was really just like home, except that there was no fig-tree, but there was a small, square yard for Trottemenu outside it and she felt very proud standing in it all alone. 'Just like a horse in its stable,' she said.

But now she stood there and shivered with fear. It was getting dark, too, and still those three strange men stood up there on the hill, staring down. She looked up at the silver star, their own star, that still shone above them, and she felt comforted, and when she looked back at the hill the figures were gone.

Some one was coming down the street, coming right towards the house. She could hear a clatter, then a strange, soft padding noise, then some one else coming 'clack-clack, clacketty-clack' close behind. It was growing darker and darker and the opening into her yard was all blocked up with dim shapes. Her knees knocked together and she put her ears right back.

'How can I warn Mary and Joseph?' she wondered, desperately. She tried to bray, but it stuck in her throat and only a ridiculous noise like a snort came out.

Suddenly, her little yard was quite full of strange animals. In pranced an enormous Horse, his hoofs right up in the air above Trottemenu's head. Even in the darkness, she saw that he shone like silver and that his mane and tail flew out like silver fountains, and all over his back he had spots like great silver pennies. In he clattered, without so much as saying 'please.' Before she had recovered from the shock, there was a sort of shuffling noise, a loud cough, and a very grumbling voice which said.

'Ahem! Ahem! I suppose we *are* meant to go in here?'

In there trudged a great, brown Camel, sticking his long neck up to peer over the wall, and not looking at all pleased.

'Ahem!' he said. 'It's very small. I'd far rather stay out in the open.'

They pushed and shoved against Trottemenu without taking the slightest notice of her, and she thought it was very rude of them to treat her like that in her own yard.

'Please don't lean against me,' said the Horse.

'I can't help it,' answered the Camel, 'it's Abyad coming in.'

'What! Another of them?' thought Trottemenu.

And in came a creature she didn't know at all. He was a little like the Horse and a little like herself, and he was beautifully, dazzlingly white all over.

'Well! Here we all are!' he said, cheerfully, and Trottemenu decided at once that she liked him.

'Hush!' said the Horse. 'Here are our Riders.'

Three men in long, dark cloaks came in, and Trottemenu decided that if they were robbers she couldn't possibly shout for help, because she was so squashed in. Her nose was pressed almost flat against the Camel's side so that she very nearly stopped breathing. She looked round out of the corner of her eye and she saw an extraordinary thing.

Mary had just lit the lamp and hung it up on a hook in the wall, so that it threw a faint light outside. By that light the three mysterious strangers were taking off their cloaks.

They stood there, tall and foreign looking. The first one had a beautiful, kind face, and his hair and beard were as silvery-white as the Horse's mane. The second one was younger, and he had thick, curly hair; and the third one was the youngest of all. with sparkling black eyes, black hair, cheeks as brown as nuts, and flashing gold rings in his ears. They stood in a line and each one lifted something from his saddle-bag. Then up went their arms, there was a rustle of silk clothing exactly like birds flying, and each stranger placed on his head a crown of dazzling gold.

'Kings!' whispered Trottemenu to herself. 'Kings! Three beautiful, strange Kings!'

Each King gave a word of command to his animal in a foreign language that she did not understand, and each animal bowed his head in obedience in turn. Then the Kings turned and went silently out towards the house door.

'Could you please . . .? I mean, would you mind . . .? I am

getting so squashed, Gentlemen,' said Trottemenu, nervously, wriggling about.

'Dear me,' said the Horse, looking down at her, 'I didn't notice you.'

'Ahem! I thought I felt something,' said the Camel.

The white creature only laughed.

'What exactly are you?' asked the Horse.

'I'm Trottemenu the Donkey,' she said, in a very small voice.

'Oh! A Donkey. Yes, I have seen them about, of course.'

She felt a very small Donkey when they all stared at her so curiously.

'Ahem!' began the Camel, who always coughed before he spoke. 'We don't use them very much in my country.'

'No,' said the Horse. 'They're not very much use, I'm afraid.'

'Indeed I am!' cried Trottemenu indignantly. 'I carried Mary on my back all the way to Bethlehem.'

'What!' said the Horse, really astonished. 'Surely no one could ride YOU!'

They all stared at her again, and now Trottemenu felt like the very smallest Donkey in all the world. She felt all ears. But the kindly white animal edged up close and whispered,

'Don't take any notice of them. My Mother was a Donkey.'

Then he added, aloud,

'Perhaps, at any rate, we ought to introduce ourselves. After all, we are in some one else's stable.'

'Stable!' snorted the Camel, under his breath.

'Certainly,' said the Horse, in a very dignified way. 'It shall never be said that a true Arab steed forgot his manners. My name is Sari. I am one of the fastest horses in Arabia. I move like a flash of light, and no man can catch me but my Master. I have never yet worn a bridle. When he wishes me to turn, he has only to touch my neck with his knee.'

'Ahem! Hrrmp! Grrmp!' said the Camel, clearing his throat several times. 'Allow me to present myself. Abu Tazammur, at your service. Possibly I am not so fast as my friend here, but I can travel for days across the sands with only a small handful of thistle to eat. I can smell water more than a mile away and guide my Master to it.'

'As for me,' said the white creature, 'I'm Abyad the Mule. I don't pretend to be as valuable as you two, but I love my Master and he loves me, and I don't get tired however far we go.'

A shadow suddenly fell across the window, and they all edged themselves round and looked over the low wall. By twisting their necks to one side they could see right into the room of the house. Even little Trottemenu could see over Abyad's shoulder. It was just like being at a play, to watch what was happening.

There was Joseph, looking over Mary's shoulder, and on her knee sat the Baby Jesus, laughing and crowing with delight, his downy black hair all rumpled up because he had just woken up from sleep. As the animals watched, holding their breath, the Stranger Kings went one by one past the window, three glistening golden crowns bobbing past in the lamplight.

'Lovely, lovely, lovely!' sang Trottemenu, in a funny, excited, croaky voice.

'Please don't make that extraordinary noise,' said Abu Tazammur, but Trottemenu was far too excited to take any notice.

She could see now that the Stranger Kings were all dressed in silk. The first one was in a colour like the sea, sometimes blue and sometimes green, with flashings like emeralds in the folds. The second was dressed like the sunset, all orange and flame and scarlet; but the third King was in cloth-of-gold, woven just like a great golden cobweb.

Each one went in turn up to Jesus and laid a present before him, bowing very low as he offered it.

The first King gave him a golden box carved with a hundred

different golden flowers. The second King gave him a blue china jar with holes like lace in the sides to let the sweet smells out. The third King only gave him a plain black box.

'Oh dear, oh dear!' sighed Trottemenu, very disappointed. 'That last present doesn't look very exciting. It isn't a bit like the others.'

Abyad the Mule uttered a deep sigh.

'No,' he said, very sadly. 'My Rider has carried that box a long, long way under my saddle. It has a very bitter spice inside it, and perhaps it means that the tiny King will be unhappy one day.'

'He shan't be if I can help it,' said Trottemenu, bravely. 'I'm going to look after him.'

'Ahem! Excuse me,' said Abu Tazammur the Camel, peering over Abyad's shoulder, 'I don't wish to be inquisitive, I'm sure, but . . .'

'Oh, please don't apologize,' said Trottemenu, politely, wondering why his manner had so suddenly changed.

'I only wanted to know,' Abu Tazammur went on, 'if you really belong here.'

'Of course I do. Those are my Owners in there.'

'Really!' said Sari the Horse, in a very interested way. 'Perhaps we ought to apologize. You see, we did not understand at first. We are very special animals because the Three Kings ride us, but we didn't know it was a King that we were coming to see, a tiny King in a tiny house.

'He must be a very great King for all he is so little,' said Aybad, softly.

'I've never seen my Rider bow down so low before,' added Abu Tazammur.

'Nor I.'

'Nor I.'

They all turned and stared at Trottemenu, and this time she did not feel at all a small Donkey and she forgot how shaggy and grey she was. She only felt very proud.

'I think he is the greatest King in the whole world,' she said, happily.

Just at that moment the three Riders came out of the house, and called in their foreign language to their steeds. Abyad was the first to go, and he trotted gaily to the opening in the wall. Next went Sari, giving a funny little neigh of welcome to his Master, and, last of all, Abu Tazammur shuffled along, his big, clumsy feet scuffling over the ground and grumpy little grumbling noises rumbling all up his long throat. At the door they turned and looked over their shoulders.

'Good-bye,' said Abyad the Mule, 'and don't forget what I told you about my Mother.'

'No, I won't,' promised Trottemenu, 'and thank you very much.'

'Good-bye,' said Sari the Horse. 'It has been a great pleasure to meet you.'

'Ahem! Ahrrmp!' coughed Abu Tazammur the Camel. 'I must say that things aren't always what they seem. Perhaps I was a little bit . . . er . . . hasty when I came in. If so, I apologize.'

'Oh, please don't,' said Trottemenu. 'I have enjoyed meeting you all.'

Sari and Abyad and Abu Tazammur then bowed to her very courteously, all three of them, and went outside to their Riders.

Trottemenu stood with her head on one side, listening. She heard the three Riders mount, then one of them gave a low, clear whistle, like a bird, and away they went up the dark street. She heard Sari bounding along on his great hoofs, Abyad trotting merrily after, and Abu Tazammur padding and scuffling behind. The last sound she heard was a smothered 'Ahem!' floating back in the darkness.

She stood all alone in her little yard. Joseph moved the lamp so that there was only a very dim light in the room in the house. Trottemenu looked up at the silver star and sighed deeply with happiness. Then her head drooped, her eyes closed, and she fell asleep, dreaming wonderful dreams of silver horses with shining spots like moons all over their backs and long silver manes, of gold crowns and stars and boxes of strange spice.

CHAPTER SIX

In which they run away by night

SHE STOOD THERE, her head niddy-nodding with sleep. It was quite silent in the town, for every one had gone to bed. Suddenly, in the silence, a voice whispered in her ear.

'Trottemenu! Trottemenu! Wake up!'

'Oh dear, oh dear,' she sighed, 'I must be still dreaming.'

'Wake up!' said the voice. 'Hush, don't make a sound.' She blinked her eyes and twitched her ears. Then she wrinkled up her velvety nose and smelt that it was Joseph standing close to her in the dark, his hand on her neck.

What could be the matter? Her heart began to thump against her ribs.

'Hush!' said Joseph again. 'Don't move.'

She snuggled against him to show that she had understood, and he pulled her ear close up against his mouth and began to whisper into it. It was rather tickly, but she kept quite still and listened.

'You mustn't make a single sound,' said Joseph in a very low voice. 'We are going to run away. I have had a terrible dream to-night. I was lying on my mat, sound asleep, when I thought an Angel came and touched me, and woke me up. I sat up with a start and I seemed to see an awful thing. I saw the wicked old King Herod coming to kill our Baby Jesus.'

Trottemenu wanted to laugh, it sounded so absurd. She often had dreams, and only just now she had been dreaming about silver Sari and his Rider, but she didn't get up in the middle of the night and run away. However, Joseph sounded very serious and she could feel that he was trembling all over under his brown coat.

'You must come to the door of the house on tip-toe,' he went on. 'You must be very careful not to step on any loose stones, or to make even as much sound as a mouse.'

So she followed him out in the dark because she had made the Donkey Promise of Obedience to him, and stood at the door, still hanging her head down very sleepily and twitching her ears. All in silence, rather frightening, Mary came to the door with their sleeping-mats rolled up into tidy bundles, and Joseph brought out her little saddle and bridle. How still they stood, listening, when the bridle gave a little chink! Then the linen bags of biscuit and raisins and a small bottle of wine were tied on.

'There's nothing ready for Trottemenu to take to eat on the way,' whispered Mary.

'Then she will have to make do with grass and leaves until we can get her something,' Joseph whispered back.

'It must be very serious after all,' thought Trottemenu, 'although it does seem very odd.'

They were off. Mary was riding, and, wrapped in her big, blue cloak, she carried the Baby Jesus, cuddled up tight. He thought it was great fun and peeped out of his wrappings with bright eyes, like a young bird from under its mother's wing. They left the lamp burning so that people should think they were still there, and that was how they stole away from the little white house in Bethlehem in the middle of the night, and they never went back there any more.

Trottemenu went on the tips of her hoofs, padding along so silently that the people sleeping in all the houses they passed never heard her go by. Soon they were out of the town, and still they went on and on, and the sun rose and they were still travelling. It was hot, and still they went, looking over their shoulders every time they heard any one coming, going very quickly past every clump of trees in case Herod's soldiers were hiding behind it with their daggers to catch them, and kill the Little King. They had only very short stops for meals, and then Trottemenu had to go nosing all around the ground for little tufts of grass to eat, and twigs off the trees, for Joseph said that she could break the Picking and Snatching Rule until they could get her something.

For three whole weeks they travelled like that, sleeping under the stars, cuddled up together for warmth, and going on again as soon as the sun rose. How tired and stiff they were getting! To make matters worse, the country grew worse and worse. There were no trees, hardly any houses, only miles and miles of sand, all humped up and down in little hills. It blew into their eyes and their hair, and crept into all their clothes and into the biscuit-bread they carried and into Trottemenu's rough coat and furry ears. Mary wrapped Jesus up as well as she could against it, and he slept nearly all the way.

They passed some men ploughing in the sand, strange, brown-faced men with shining black eyes and white clothes. They spoke a greeting to them and hurried on, and the men stared curiously at them.

Once Trottemenu saw something that made her laugh. She saw these men ploughing with a little donkey, no bigger than herself, and a big, knobbly-kneed camel yoked together in the plough.

'Just as if Abu Tazammur and I went to work together,' she said to herself. 'Wouldn't he grumble and mutter and say "Ahem!" if he had to go to work with me!' And the idea so amused her that she opened her mouth wide and laughed—

'Hee-haw, ha! ha!'

'Hurry!' said Joseph, anxiously. 'Hurry! Hurry on!'

They came to a well in the sand, and had to stop to drink. It was not a bit like any well that they had ever seen before. There was a long stick in the ground with another one tied across it at the top, like a letter 'T'. On one arm of it hung a bucket, tied by a rope, and they had to pull it up. Trottemenu saw a very strange plant growing near the well. It looked like a chain of green circles growing out of each other, and it smelt quite juicy and carrotty, but when she crunched it up she found that she had a mouthful of prickles.

'Brrrrr!' she said, and spat it out.

'That's a cactus,' said Joseph, laughing at her disgusted face.

As they were resting and drinking the clear, cold water, they saw a little cloud of dust up the road by which they had come.

Joseph jumped up, but already a man was in sight, galloping along on a mule. It was no use running away. The man was already flinging himself off and coming to the well.

'Peace be with you!' he said.

'And with you, peace,' answered Joseph, politely, but taking care to stand in front of Mary, who had Jesus hidden right inside her cloak.

'Where are you going, so far from a town?' the stranger asked curiously.

'We are making our way into Egypt,' explained Joseph, 'and already we must be going on.'

He was wondering desperately if the man had a knife hidden under his cloak. He didn't see at all how he could find out.

The stranger began to walk towards Mary.

'What are you hiding under your cloak?' he demanded, staring at her.

They thought all was lost. Then, just as he put out his hand to pull Mary's cloak aside, something hit him violently behind his knees and he sat down with a terrible bump in the sand.

'Well!' he said, beginning to laugh. 'That has never happened to me in my whole life before,' and he picked himself up and began to rub behind his knees where Trottemenu's hard, bony little head had butted him so rudely.

'What a fierce little animal! I see she means to protect you. And now aren't you going to let me have a look at the little boy you have hidden away there?'

They were terrified, and Trottemenu bared her teeth to bite him, in spite of all the Donkey Laws, but the stranger went straight up to Mary, and, gently pulling her cloak aside, he smiled down at the little, sunburnt face of Jesus.

'You will soon be safe,' he said. 'You were wise to come. There is not a baby left alive in the whole town of Bethlehem. He has killed them all, and last night every one in all the streets was kept awake by the mothers weeping for their little children.'

Mary's eyes filled with tears and even Joseph had to turn away. No children to laugh and play anywhere!

'Go on now,' said the stranger, 'and before many hours you will come to the river. On the other side of it you will be in Egypt and King Herod cannot touch you. I must stay here a while to rest my mule, but here are a few dates to refresh you.'

How they thanked him! And Trottemenu rubbed her face against his coat to apologize for having knocked him over, so that he quite understood and laughed at her.

They went on, half happy and half sad. It was sunny, and not too hot. Early in the afternoon Joseph shaded his eyes and looked ahread, then he suddenly gave a great shout.

'Trees!' he shouted. 'Palm trees! The river is there.'

On they raced, tired as they were, until they came to the river. There it lay, cool and shining, like a piece of silver ribbon threaded through the sand, and under the palm trees it was cool and shady. There was a special shallow place built up with white stones where they had to cross, so over they went, the four of them, and down to the bank on the other side.

They were safe! Herod could not reach them. They laughed and they shouted, they ate dates and paddled in the shallow water near the bank. Jesus suddenly sat up and crowed like a cock for fun, and they all laughed again, and Joseph picked Him up and sat Him right up on his shoulder, and away they all marched happily to find a real shelter for the coming night.

CHAPTER SEVEN

In which they return Home

THE PEOPLE OF EGYPT seemed very strange to them after their own people. However hard Trottemenu listened, she could not understand what they said. They had slanting black eyes and brown skins and very straight black hair, and they wore strange clothes, too, very short and nearly always white. Sometimes they had queer little patterns on them, but no wide, gay stripes of orange and red and bright green such as the people in their own land had.

'Still,' said Joseph, 'we came here to be safe from the wicked King Herod, and one day we may be able to go home again.'

They lived by the shore of a beautiful lake shaded by palm trees, and it was not very long before Joseph found some work to do, making wooden ploughs for the little donkeys and the camels to pull, and seats for boats, for the Egyptian people were very fond of rowing. Trottemenu found it very queer to walk on dry sand after stony roads, and at first she trod so carefully that her little hoofs sank right in and made deep holes, and then she could hardly pull them out again. 'Squelch—squelch,' they went, and then 'Hissssss' as the loose sand slithered down into the hole again.

'Ho! Ho!' shouted an old brown Camel, watching her, and laughing, with his long neck stretched out and his lips curled back to show all his yellow teeth. 'You'll never get anywhere like that.'

'But what can I do?' asked poor Trottemenu.

'Well, for one thing, your feet aren't big enough. You want big, sensible pads like mine.'

And he lifted one up and waved it proudly in the air.

'But what can I do? I'm sure mine won't grow any more now.'

Trottemenu was very worried. The old Camel thought deeply for a minute, then he said:

'You could try stepping very lightly and quickly, sort of skimming over the top. Like this.'

Off he set, lumbering along and wobbling from side to side his rather small head bobbing and dipping on his long neck, looking so comical that Trottemenu had to bite her lips to keep from laughing out loud.

'Thank you very much,' she said, meekly, 'I'll try it.'

She soon succeeded quite well, and she went trotting so lightly and swiftly over the sand that she hardly left the tiniest dent behind.

She had not very much work to do in Egypt, so she used to stand in the shade of the palm trees and watch Jesus at play. He could walk now, and he would take little, toddling steps and then break into a run. He loved the silvery waves that rippled up onto the edge of the sand when the wind blew, and he always tried to run towards them, so that, if he came too near, Trottemenu had to take the back of his tunic between her velvety lips and give him a gentle tug backwards. Sometimes he tried to talk, and then Trottemenu made funny little noises in the back of her throat to encourage him, and that made him gurgle with laughter, and then Mary would come out to see what they were doing and she would laugh, too, to hear them trying to talk to each other.

One day, very early in the morning, Trottemenu was standing under a tree, watching the sunrise. First of all, the sky was pale green, like a piece of glass, then it turned gold, then red, and all the little waves on the lake turned red, too, and all the ripples in the sand. She was so interested in this that she did not hear Joseph come out of the house.

'Well, Little Friend,' he said, putting his arm round her, so that she felt warm all through with pride. 'What do you think has happened? We are going home. We are really going home.'

She wanted to ask if it was really safe to take Jesus back, but she couldn't think how to do it, but Joseph must have guessed, for he went on:

'While I was asleep last night, I heard a voice saying, "Joseph, King Herod is dead. Go back home. Herod is dead." When I opened my eyes, I just caught a glimpse of the same Angel who came before. I only just saw the flash of his wings, but I'm sure it will be quite safe for us to go.'

How different it was from their other journey! They laughed and talked and made a great clatter with their packing, and called out jokes to their friends. They wished every one good-bye before they set out, and then they sat Jesus up on the saddle, with Mary walking beside him to hold him on. Away they went, all of them singing a song that went—

'When Israel came out of Egypt
And from among the strange people . . .'

It was a very old song, and even Trottemenu was able to add some odd noises in an undertone.

The journey seemed very short because they marched along so happily every day. They didn't mind the heat, or the sand, and they kept reminding each other of the things they had passed on the way down.

'Do you remember the man at the well, Mary?'

'Yes, and the dates he gave me.'

'And we thought he was hiding a knife or a dagger!'

And when they passed through Bethlehem,

'There's the little house where we used to live!'

'I wonder if some one lives there now?'

'And there's the khan where Jesus came to us!'

Trottemenu turned her head to look, and who should be standing in the yard but Mâchellant! He lumbered to the gate and gave them a friendly bellow, and Trottemenu laughed and flicked her ears gaily at him.

'Why! There's the very same old brown Ox!' cried Joseph, and Jesus stretched out His arms to him.

On went Trottemenu, never tiring, 'clicketty, clack-clack,' her little, shiny hoofs twinkling in and out.

They were home. They really were home again. Down the steep main street of Nazareth they came, their long journey over. There was the little white house, just as they had left it. There was the fig-tree, all in leaf, but it had grown quite a foot taller. They ran in and out, unpacking their possessions, excited to be back.

'There's my orange mat that I left behind,' said Mary, 'and the little water-pot still standing by the big water-pot, and the corn-mill, and my baking stone.'

'And my tools haven't rusted,' said Joseph, 'and—look! There are even the little, yellow curls of wood left over from the box I was making!'

'And there's my special ring in the wall,' said Trottemenu, to herself.

It was lovely to be home in summer. They never shut the door of the house, and Trottemenu could stand under her tree and watch Mary making flat cakes of bread from ground corn and water and baking them on a hot stone. She could see Jesus helping her in the house, rolling up the sleeping mats tidily and putting them away in a corner, trying to sweep with a broom much too big for him. Mary made him a little, round, red cap to keep the sun from his head, and he went to market with her and Trottemenu, looking exactly like a ripe, rosy apple, with his sunburnt cheeks and his red cap bobbing up and down. He went to the well with Mary, too, but he wasn't big enough yet to lift the big, stone water-pots.

In the afternoons it was far too hot for him to go outside, so he generally pulled out his mat and lay down inside the house. Mary would sit by him and sing, and, gradually, his eyelids would grow droopier and droopier, and he would be asleep.

Trottemenu loved Mary's song for Jesus, 'It just shows,' she thought, 'that he really is a King, although he is so tiny.'

And the notes of Mary's lullaby would float through the window, clear and sweet as a bird's song. And this is what she sang—

'Dear Jesus, my little King,
  Asleep in the sun,
The whole earth is whispering,
  Till Thy sleep is done.

No sparrow is chirruping,
  No fig-leaf shall move,
To wake Thee from slumbering,
  My King and my Love.'

CHAPTER EIGHT

About six little Birds

JESUS GREW into such a jolly little boy, always happy and laughing. His legs and arms were burnt to the colour of nuts, and when he wore his scarlet tunic over a white shirt and his little scarlet cap he seemed to dance about like a flame. About this time, too, Trottemenu noticed a very odd thing. Round his head there always seemed to be a circle of light flickering, very faint, almost like a misty gold crown, and she wondered if any one else ever saw it.

'It must be because he's really a King,' she thought.

He helped Joseph as well as Mary now, and put away the tools tidily on the shelf and collected all the little shavings of wood to light the fire. He loved to play with Trottemenu, stroking her and giving her little pieces of bread to eat, but he was not tall enough to get on her back.

'If he can't reach me,' she thought, 'then clearly I must make myself smaller.'

So she went down on her knees and knelt in front of Jesus, and he scrambled on and held her shaggy mane while she carefully stood up again. Then they went proudly up to the door.

'How did you get up there?' cried Mary, laughing, and Trottemenu, delighted with her own cleverness, trotted gently up and down in front of the house with Jesus on her back.

When he was five, on his birthday, she decided to give him a very special ride, right up the road, and Mary said they might go if they were very careful.

It was such fun, cantering along all by themselves, and all the other boys stared at them. They went right to the edge of the Market, and Jesus wasn't a bit afraid because he knew perfectly well that Trottemenu wouldn't let him fall off, whatever happened.

From under a tree in the Square a group of boys called out—'Happy birthday, Jesus.'

'Thank you,' he answered.

'Aren't you coming to play with us?'

'What at?'

Trottemenu carried him near so that he could see. They had some big lumps of clay that they had taken out from the sides of the well, all wet and sticky, and they were making animals with it.

'Look at my camel,' said little Reuben.

'I don't think it's much like a camel,' answered Benjamin, looking at it. 'It looks more like an old tree.'

'It IS a camel!' persisted Reuben, but when he held it up for them to look at, its long neck dropped off and they all laughed.

'Guess what mine is,' said Amos.

'An elephant!' said one.

'A little house!' said another.

'A funny old man!' said a third.

'Don't be silly,' said Amos. 'It's the little mouse that crept into our corn bin last night.'

'You come and make one, Jesus,' Benjamin said.

'Yes,' said the others, 'let's give him the biggest lump of clay because it's his birthday, and watch what he makes.'

Jesus didn't quite know whether he ought to stay and play, but Trottemenu knelt down obligingly for him to slip off, so he thought it must be all right.

His quick fingers took the clay and shaped it so swiftly that they hardly saw them move.

'He's making little birds!' shouted Aaron, excitedly. 'Little birds just like real! Look at their wings!'

Jesus put them down one by one, six little sparrows, complete from their sharp beaks to their pointed claws. One of them even had its wings spread out as if it were just going to fly, and you could see all the feathers along the edges.

They were delighted. They clapped their hands and shouted so that two men coming from the Market paused to see what they were all doing and what all the noise was about.

'I'm going to make some,' Benjamin said.

'Give me a piece of clay to try.' Amos and Reuben both took a piece at the same time so that it broke in two.

There they all squatted in the dust, each one pudging his dirty fingers in the clay, some of them getting it on their faces as well. And, truth to tell, the birds they made were a very funny collection. Some of them had big heads and little bodies, and some had big bodies and little tiny heads. Benjamin's bird had a crooked beak, and Amos's had only one wing, because, he said, Reuben had taken the bigger piece of clay, and he hadn't enough to finish it with. While he was explaining this to them, the one wing fell off into the dust and Benjamin accidentally put his foot on it.

They argued and chattered, as boys will, and Jesus knelt behind them, smiling and playing with his six little clay sparrows. Trottemenu was watching him. As his fingers stroked them, one little sparrow blinked. Its eyes came open like jewels, gold and twinkling. Another little sparrow opened its beak and shut it again. The one with outspread wings suddenly flapped them, and stretched. All along their backs downy feathers pushed through the clay, and soon there were six fluffy little birds hopping up and down on the road. One little rascal even pecked cheekily at a grain of chaff.

Then 'Chip, chip, che-e-ep!' they all said. There was a rustle of wings, a fanning of the air, and then nothing at all on the road but dust.

'It's no good,' Amos said, 'I can't do it. Let's look again at the ones Jesus made, and see how he did it. Why, where are they?'

They all turned and stared.

'They've gone!'

Jesus stood up.

'They all flew away,' he said, laughing. 'Never mind, I'll come again another day and make you some more to take home with you.'

Trottemenu knelt down for him to mount, and they went home together, chuckling, but they never told any one, not even Mary, about the six little clay sparrows who had spread their wings and flown away.

CHAPTER NINE

In which Jesus is lost

JESUS GREW tall and strong, and to Trottemenu he seemed the most Beautiful Person in the world. She was quite sure that no other Donkey had a Master like hers, or ever had. She used to wonder why he had to go to school with the other boys, for she thought that he knew everything that there was to know; but go to school he did. He and Reuben and Amos and Benjamin and all the others ran off every morning together. In school they sat on the floor in a ring round the schoolmaster, and they learnt their letters by chanting them over and over again, rocking their bodies backwards and forwards at the same time. Once it was so hot and they chanted in such a sing-song way that little Reuben rolled over on the floor, sound asleep, and they had to pick him up and shake him.

Jesus was twelve. He came running out of the house, full of exciting news.

'What do you think?' He called out. 'This year I'm old enough to go to Jerusalem with all the grown-ups! Just think! I shall see Jerusalem!'

Trottemenu did not think it anything so very wonderful. She had heard of it, of course, for Joseph and Mary went every year, but they always went in a waggon with their relations. However, she hoped very much that they would take her this year, as Jesus was going. She had stayed quietly at home for a long time, now, and perhaps a little holiday away, meeting other animals, would be a pleasant change.

As the time to go drew near, the whole town began to get

ready, all the grown-up people and all the donkeys and the few camels who lived in Nazareth. Even the little boys who were not going ran about getting in every one's way, offering to carry bundles of mats and rugs and then strapping them onto the backs of the wrong Donkeys.

It was a lovely Spring day when they started out at last, sunny, with a little cool wind blowing the clouds about. Even the fig-tree was pushing out tiny green leaves like five fingers against the wall, and you could smell a leafy smell in the air. What a gathering there was! There seemed hundreds of Donkeys, grey and brown and creamy-white, all tossing their shaggy heads and stamping their tiny hoofs with impatience. Most of them had new saddles of yellow or red, and, at the very last minute, Joseph came hurrying out with a brand-new one of shiny scarlet leather for Trottemenu. She had a little silver bell, too, tied in the middle of her forehead, and when she went near other Donkeys she kept shaking her head to make it jingle. The camels were stretching their long necks in every direction, coughing and grunting and grumbling, but really just as pleased as any one else to be going. Some little children had to come, too, because there was no one to leave at home to look after them.

There was such a noise when they moved off. People shouted advice, donkeys brayed with excitement, the ox-carts creaked and rumbled, and all the cooking pots and pans clattered and clashed and banged and rattled. If you listened very carefully you could hear through it all the chiming of the little bells that the camels wore tied round their necks. All through the long, sunny day they travelled, and when night came they stopped and unfolded their tents.

It was strange and almost like a game, sleeping in tents and eating supper cooked over a camp fire. One by one the children grew sleepy and were rolled in rugs by their mothers and carried away to bed. Soon it was quite silent everywhere, except for the steady munching of grass where the animals were, for nothing is more delicious after a hot, dusty journey than grass with the dew on it.

On the third day they began to draw near Jerusalem. Every one began to whisper and look ahead.

'Jerusalem! Jerusalem!' they whispered, and it made a noise

like dry leaves rustling as the whisper passed all down the line.

Then they began to sing. The road went uphill, and they had special songs called the Climbing Songs. At first it was very faint, then it came swelling out, great waves of song, queer Jewish music that was sad and gay at the same time. The caravan was so long by now that the verses the leaders sung floated back to those behind and they were singing quite a different verse. Puffs of song came floating back like clouds.

'I was glad when they said unto me,
We will go into the House of the Lord,
Our feet shall stand in thy gates,
O Jerusalem.'

Then there was a pause, and, all at once, a boy began playing, on a flute. Sweet and shrill and piercing as a robin's song in winter, it floated down the line.

And then there was the deep singing of the men again:

'O pray for the peace of Jerusalem,
They shall prosper that love thee.
Peace be within thy walls
And plenteousness within thy palaces.'

'I can see it! I can see it!' cried Jesus, flinging one arm over Trottemenu's neck.

People at the front of the line all began to call out, and the shout grew louder and louder until it was like thunder.

'Jerusalem!'

'Jerusalem!'

'JERUSALEM!'

Everybody stopped. In front of them the mist lay on the ground like a white sea, and out of it Jerusalem rose like a fairy-tale island. There were terraces above terraces, roofs and domes and palaces of snowy marble and glittering gold, streets and houses all shining, and above everything, like a great glittering bubble, the Temple itself.

On and on they pushed, every one laughing and jostling in the streets. There was plenty of room for every one, and stables for all the animals, and they had a very pleasant time of it. Trottemenu shared her stall with a dear little brown Donkey who had brought a mother and father and a small boy, younger than Jesus, to Jerusalem. The two of them chatted together for hours, sharing their barley and dried grass at meal times, politely pressing the last mouthful on each other. Every morning they were awakened just before dawn by the great peal of silver trumpets from the Temple, and then they stood up and yawned and flicked ears and stretched and hoped that their Owners were enjoying everything as much as they were.

They were quite sorry to part when Joseph came for Trottemenu, and each said that she hoped to meet the other again one day.

There were not so many people going back, for some of them were staying for a whole week instead of only three days, and

so they went more slowly. Joseph was right away at the front of the line, with men he had met in Jerusalem, and Mary walked right behind, talking to her cousins. Trottemenu could just see Joseph going on ahead when there happened to be a straight piece of road. But where was Jesus?

It seemed very strange that he was not walking at her side, chattering away and telling her all about it. All day she worried and wondered. Surely he would come running up in a minute. But he did not come.

It began to grow towards evening. There was something very, very wrong.

'I know there is,' said Trottemenu. 'I won't go on until I find out.'

She suddenly stopped dead and dug in her hoofs and refused to budge.

'Get on, get on,' grumbled an old camel, behind her. 'Can't you see you're stopping everybody?'

'Come along, can't you? Or is there a stone in your hoof?' asked a younger camel in front of her.

'I've lost my Owner,' said Trottemenu, miserably.

'Well, he's somewhere about. He's probably walking behind.'

'I won't budge until I've seen him,' she said, obstinately.

'Get on there! Get on, can't you?' shouted a man, and hit at her with a stick. Still she stuck fast.

'We're all held up!' cried another man, running up.

Soon there was a crowd round her. They pulled at her, and pushed, and beat her, but she absolutely refused to budge an inch.

'Whose Donkey is she?' asked one.

'She belongs to Joseph Bar-Jacob, I think.'

'Call him, then, and see if she'll move for him.'

'Joseph!' they began to call. 'Joseph!'

The shout was passed all down the line, and Joseph came running back, and Mary came running from the other end of the caravan, and when they saw Trottemenu's miserable little face, they knew immediately what was the matter.

Jesus was lost. They searched everywhere. They asked every one. They looked in the waggons. He was not anywhere. No one had seen him.

It was the most dreadful moment of Trottemenu's life.

'I thought he was with you,' said Mary.

'And I thought he was with you,' said Joseph.

'We must go back.'

'Yes, we must go back and look for him.'

They drew Trottemenu out of the long line, and, anxiously, they turned round and set off back to Jerusalem. They hardly spoke a word. They did not stop to rest. All through the night they walked on, so miserable that they did not know what to do.

For three dreadful days they searched. For three dreadful days Trottemenu stood in the stable all alone and turned her face to the wall and refused to eat. She would not even drink when they brought her a bucket of clean, fresh water.

On the third day she was standing, feeling really ill, her head hanging down, when she heard footsteps and voices outside.

In came Joseph and Mary, and between them—Jesus!

It seemed too wonderful to be true. There he was, perfectly well and smiling. She smelt his tunic all over, licked his face, a thing she did not usually do, and even butted him in her delight.

They went home very quietly, not talking very much because they had been very frightened. Jesus walked close to her, leading her, and presently he began to whisper in her ear. He began to tell her about the Temple.

'There are great courts all paved with marble,' he said. 'And the bowls and vases they use are all made of gold, and some of them have jewels all over them. There's a big altar up at one end, all made of gold, and a huge candlestick made like a tall golden tree with seven golden branches, and this part is veiled off by a silver curtain that looks just like rain falling, so that only the priests can go in there. They burn spices, and there's a lovely, strange, spicy smell in the air the whole time.'

She rubbed her nose against him as they walked, but what she was really thinking was:

'And where were you when we lost you?'

'I'm sorry you were anxious about me,' Jesus said, softly. 'After the Feast, on the third day, all the wise teachers come out on to the Terrace and talk to the people, and any one can ask them questions. You wouldn't understand everything, Trottemenu, but I seemed to hear a Voice from Heaven telling me to be there. I'm sure it was God who told me what to do. He said, "My Son, you must do my work." So, you see, I had to be obedient, and stay.'

Trottemenu sighed contentedly. She didn't really understand, but she did understand that Jesus had been lost and now he was found again, and that they were all going safely and quietly home to their own little white house with the fig-tree.

CHAPTER TEN

Which is about N'Imah the gentle

Now after this time, Trottemenu began to be very busy about her own affairs. She had a dear little daughter of her own, a baby Donkey whose coat was a paler grey than her own, and who, to be perfectly honest, was very much prettier than Trottemenu herself had been.

'I shall have to begin her lessons early,' said Trottemenu, 'so that she will grow up to be a really clever Donkey.'

So they stood together under the fig-tree and recited in loud clear voices the Donkey Laws and the Donkey Promises, so that people passing by stopped to listen, and said, not understanding what they were doing, 'What a dreadful noise!'

As soon as Trottemenu's little daughter was old enough, she trotted into market behind her Mother, and she was so gentle and so friendly to everyone on the way that they named her N'Imah the Gentle. Whenever people patted her, she would rub her nose against their coats and give a funny little grunt of pleasure at the back of her throat.

One day, when N'Imah was three months old, her Mother said to her,

'Now, N'Imah, I have something very important to say to you. Stand up there, in the shade, and listen very carefully to what I am going to tell you.'

So M'Imah stood up against the house wall and cocked up her big ears and tried to look very intelligent, and Trottemenu began to tell her all about the Angel who had come out of the sky right down to the field where N'Imah's Grandmother had been standing.

'I don't really understand it,' said Trottemenu, 'but I want you to remember this:

The Little Grey Donkey shall be a King's playfellow,
And her Daughter shall see wonderful things;
But the Snow-White Donkey shall carry the King in his Triumph,
And every one shall laugh and sing.

Now say those lines after me, and never forget them.'

So N'Imah obediently said them, although she was very puzzled by them.

'But who is the Snow-White Donkey?' she asked, wrinkling up her forehead.

'We don't know yet,' answered Trottemenu, 'but I expect we shall one day.'

'And what wonderful things am I going to see?'

'Wait and see,' said her Mother.

'Well, I've seen our house and the fig-tree, and I've seen even the Market Place. What else can there be?'

'A great many things,' said Trottemenu, wisely. 'One day you will have to go away from here, and perhaps you will become a great traveller.'

'Then I'd like to see barley growing in a field. Does it really grow on stalks like grass?'

Sure enough, when N'Imah was six months old, she began her travels. A stranger came one day to the little white house in Nazareth, and spent a long time in the carpenter's shop. When he came out, he was carrying an armful of wooden plough yokes, and Joseph came with him, and they were talking together like old friends.

'You have a long way to go, Jonas,' Joseph said. 'Over twenty miles before you are home.'

'We shall go slowly,' said Jonas, 'and stop many times on the way. A merchant has things to buy and sell all along the road. I must buy olives, and when I get down to the Lake there will

be smoked fish to get; but I would come more than twenty miles to get plough yokes made by Joseph. Every one knows that they are the best in the land.'

Joseph smiled at that, and, just at that moment, Jesus came running out of the workshop, carrying a wooden box carved all over. On the lid a family of beautiful deer were leaping, with a baby deer running beside them.

'See!' said Jesus. 'I have just this minute finished it. Please take it.'

The stranger was still looking at the box with wonder when Joseph said, 'You must come inside and have a little wine and some bread and honey before you go.'

When they had gone into the house together, Jesus went over to Trottemenu and put his arms round her neck.

'Your little N'Imah must go away now,' He said. 'But you must not mind. Jonas is a kind man, or we would not let him take her. All young things have to leave home when they begin to grow up, and one day I shall have to go out into the world, too.'

N'Imah was very excited when she heard that she was to go away with Jonas, and so proud that she hardly minded leaving her Mother at all. Jonas came out and took her by her leather halter, and they said good-bye to Jesus and Mary and Joseph and Trottemenu, and they set off, Jonas carrying the plough yokes and the box, because N'Imah was rather small and had not carried much yet.

First of all, they went down to the Market Place where Jonas had left all his goods. There they found two elderly grey Donkeys called Jemimah and Tirzah waiting for them, all ready to set out for home. Jonas strapped the yokes onto Jemimah's back, but the precious box he carried himself.

'Home, now,' he said, and they all clattered out of the town, down the steep street, and out into the pretty green valley.

'Why! You're only a baby!' said Tirzah to N'Imah. 'I should think you've never been away from your Mother before.'

'Never mind,' said Jemimah, looking over her shoulder, 'you tread in our footsteps and we will look after you.'

The road was very stony in places, and there were hills, but all round them were green woods of oak trees and silvery woods of olive trees. When they had been travelling for over two hours, they came to the Lake. It rippled just like the sea, and sailing over it they could see little boats with orange sails. Jonas stopped there to buy his smoked fish, and it was so late that he decided to stay at the Khan for the night. The Donkeys stayed in the courtyard and N'Imah cuddled up close between Jemimah and Tirzah so that she was quite warm and comfortable.

They set out very early next morning, as soon as the sun was up. The road went along by the side of the water all the way and they met a great many people travelling along it in all directions. Nearly everybody seemed to know Jonas.

'Dear me,' said little N'Imah, 'I *am* seeing the world. Mother said I should be a great traveller, and so I am.'

They rested in the heat of the day, and, after that, they had only been walking for another two hours when Jemimah said, 'We are nearly home.'

They all began to trot very fast then, Jemimah and Tirzah bumping their loads up and down so that Jonas had to run after them and tell them to go more slowly.

They came to Capernaum. It was much bigger than Nazareth. The Market Place seemed crowded with things to sell and with people to buy them, every one calling out and shouting at the top of his voice, asking Jonas what he had brought back from his travels and how soon he would unpack his wares.

N'Imah opened her eyes very wide and stared at everything. 'Well,' she said, 'Mother said I was to see wonderful things, and now I am seeing this enormous town.'

Even the house where Jonas lived was much bigger than any house she had ever seen before, and when she stood in the courtyard and looked through the open doorway, she knew that Jonas must be a very rich man, because he had beautiful rugs of red and blue on the floor, and even one made of real fur.

She was very happy in her new home. Jemimah and Tirzah helped her all they could, and Jonas was kind to her, and when she had no work to do, she could watch all the different people streaming along the road, and even look right beyond them at the fishermen and the boats on the Lake of Galilee, so that it was like being at the sea-side all the time.

N'Imah grew up big and strong and was able to do her share of the work with the others, to go to market and to go on long journeys with Jonas to buy goods to sell again at Capernaum. She even went back to Nazareth once or twice and told Trottemenu all the wonderful things she had seen. Jesus always had a little handful of something specially nice for her to eat when she came, and N'Imah thought that he was more beautiful and more kind every time she saw him. He was so tall and strong, with a laughing, sunburnt face, and hands that knew just where a

Donkey liked to be stroked.

In Capernaum N'Imah had a particular friend, too, some one whom she loved better than any one else. This was Deborah. Deborah lived opposite Jonas, and she used to run out every day and bring a piece of bread, or even an apple, to N'Imah, and stay and play with her. She was a very lively little girl, always skipping up and down and tossing her long, black hair out of her eyes and clapping her hands for pleasure. She wore pretty white dresses with a band of embroidery in gold and red and blue round the bottom, and a plaited gold girdle round her waist.

'She must be a very rich little girl to wear such lovely embroideries,' N'Imah said innocently to Jemimah one day.

'Why! Of course she is!' Jemimah answered. 'Her Father is the most important man in the whole of Capernaum. Haven't you seen the Ruler Jairus? He is the Ruler of the Synagogue where our Owner and all his friends go to say their prayers and to worship God.'

Deborah had just had her twelfth birthday, and there came a morning when she was late. N'Imah was looking anxiously across the road for her, and when at last she appeared, she was not skipping and jumping as usual. She walked very slowly, and, every now and then, she put her hand up to her head.

'Oh dear,' she sighed, 'I am so tired, and I have such a headache.'

N'Imah rubbed against her, but, do what she could, she could not cheer Deborah up.

The next day Deborah did not come at all, nor the next day, nor the next. Then the news was all over the town. Deborah, lively, dancing, skipping Deborah, was ill. She lay on her bed with her eyes closed and she did not even hear when people spoke to her. They took her all the best fruits they could find, figs and apples and oranges and pomegranates, but she lay quite still and did not once open her eyes. Jonas even took across the box that Jesus had made for him when he was a boy, his greatest treasure, but Deborah did not see it.

N'Imah stood miserably across the road and hung her head. Feet went hurrying by, but she did not look up.

'I shall never see Deborah again,' she said.

More and more feet went clap-clap, clap-clap, scutter-scutter on the pavement.

'Where can they all be going?' she began to wonder.

Every one in the town was running down to the Lake. Then people began to whisper, and the whisper grew and grew, and then they began to call out to each other, and the whisper was a shout.

'Jesus is coming! Jesus is coming!'

N'Imah's heart leaped up for joy. Jesus was coming! Surely he could put things right. If only she could get to him to tell him about Deborah!

As if in answer to her wish, she saw Jairus himself come to the door of the house opposite and go running off with the crowd towards the shore, just as if he were not the most important man in the town. What a crowd there was down there! She could see them all pushing and struggling to get in the front, and there was a little boat coming across the water with Jesus and his friends standing up in it. She was so busy watching that she forgot to look at the house across the road.

All at once, a servant came out and began to run. He ran straight past N'Imah and down towards the shore, and, as he ran, the tears were streaming down his face.

'Deborah is dead! Deborah is dead!' he cried, and went running on.

Then there came a terrible noise from the house. Every one cried and sobbed out loud, and some of them began wailing, and they even played sad tunes on a flute to show how unhappy they were. Still Jairus did not come back. Still the servant who had run to tell him did not come back. It seemed hours and hours and hours to the miserable N'Imah before anything happened except the dreadful noise of crying in the house opposite.

Gradually, the crowd down on the shore began to break up, and there, walking up the street with Jairus by his side and all the people following behind, was Jesus. And Jesus was smiling! He even found a minute to speak to N'Imah before he crossed the road.

He went straight across the road to Jairus' house, and by then there was even a crowd of people wailing and sobbing all round the front door.

'Why!' said Jesus, in a clear, calm voice. 'There is no need for you to weep like this. Deborah is not dead. She is only asleep.'

They did not believe him.

'Of course she's dead,' they said, and they began to be all the noisier, and some of them even laughed scornfully.

Jesus went right in at the door, and only Jairus followed him and three very special friends who had come in the boat with Jesus—Peter and James and John.

Everything was very quiet. No one spoke. No one dared to make a sound. Then a tiny rustle crept through the crowd. There was the noise of a little girl laughing.

All at once, Deborah ran down the steps, clapping her hands, her eyes sparkling with fun, her hair flying over her shoulders.

'What a crowd of people!' she cried. 'They must all have come to see Jesus. And there's my darling N'Imah looking quite sad!'

She danced across the road to her, and pulled her ears gently in fun.

'Good afternoon, N'Imah,' she said. 'We have a very important visitor to-day. Jesus has come to our house. And what do you think? I nearly missed him! I think I must have been dreaming. . . . I remember I was asleep, and, somehow, I seemed such a long, long way away, as if I'd gone on a journey. Then I seemed to hear Jesus say, "Maiden, arise!" I opened my eyes, and there he stood, right by my bed, and Mother and Father stood there, too, and—what do you think?—Mother had been crying! Wasn't that strange!'

N'Imah was so happy that she could not say anything at all, or even rub her nose against Deborah's dress. She just stood perfectly still because she was so happy.

'Well, you funny Donkey,' Deborah said, pulling her ears a little harder, 'you ARE quiet to-day. What do you think was the first thing that Jesus did when I was properly awake? He gave me an orange to eat!'

Deborah smiled mischievously, and took N'Imah's ear and whispered into it, so that it tickled.

'And if you promise not to tell any one, there is an apple for you, and I mean to bring it out to you soon.'

She dropped a kiss on the velvet tip of N'Imah's nose and ran away, laughing.

N'Imah watched her go, then she said, very solemnly,

'That's the most wonderful thing of all. What a tale I shall have to tell when I go to Nazareth again!'

CHAPTER ELEVEN

In which the snow-white Donkey is born

N'IMAH WAS SO PROUD of herself that she wanted to run out into the street and tell everybody what she had done. She had a son, and he was the most wonderful Donkey ever born into the world. He was beautifully, dazzlingly white, from the velvet tip of his nose to the tassel on the end of his little tail. They called him Laban. When N'Imah and Laban stood together outside Jonas's house, people would stop to stare over the low wall at them. Children, playing in the sand at the edge of the street, would ask each other,

'Have you seen Laban to-day?'

Then they would stop their play and run off to admire him. Deborah could hardly bear to leave him for a moment, and even Jonas was astonished at his beauty.

'Surely he will be very famous one day,' he said. 'He shall never wear a saddle or carry any bundles like an ordinary Donkey.'

Laban's coat was like silk, and when the sun shone on it each hair looked like a silver thread. His little hoofs were so new and unused to hard roads that they, too, were silvery white, just as if they had been polished, and, every morning, Deborah ran across the road carrying a soft brush, with which she brushed his silky back all over. Laban stood quite still while she did this, watching her with his big, shining eyes which were dark blue in the centres. Perhaps he knew that as soon as she had finished he would get an apple or a red, juicy carrot.

N'Imah thought and thought about Laban. She woke up in the night and looked at him, sleeping in the moonlight, to see if he was as white as she had thought he was. Of course he was. He seemed to grow whiter every day. She thought about him all the time she was out with Jemimah and Tirzah, for Jonas would not let him go with his Mother in case he became dusty or too tired on the road, or in case any one tried to steal him or hit him. When N'Imah was coming home again with a load on her back, she would trot faster and faster the nearer she drew to Capernaum, until Jemimah, who was getting rather old, and, to be perfectly truthful, a little too fat, panted behind her,

'We are not running a race, N'Imah. Tirzah and I can't keep up with you. My bundles of smoked fish are bumping up and down on my back as if they were alive again.'

'We must hurry along,' N'Imah would answer. 'I must give Laban his lessons to-night, before he goes to bed.'

She taught him all she knew, all the Laws and the Promises, and the Prophecy. She was a little frightened when she taught him the Prophecy that Trottemenu had taught her.

'The Snow-White Donkey shall carry the King in his Triumph,' she said to herself. 'It must mean Laban. I hope I am training him properly. I wish I were a more clever Donkey myself, so that I could teach him more.'

N'Imah did not know that she herself was so kind and gentle that Laban could not help growing up as good and amiable as a little Donkey could possibly be. His Mother sent a message about him to Trottemenu, and it was carried by a friend of Jemimah's, whose Owner was going to Nazareth. Trottemenu was so excited when she heard about Laban that she stood under her fig-tree and sang the Prophecy out loud in a very queer, croaky voice, because she was a very old Grandmother Donkey by now, and her coat was greyer than ever.

One day, early in spring, Jonas said to Jemimah and Tirzah and N'Imah,

'We are going on a very short journey to-day, just a few miles round the Lake, but I have some rugs to sell and you must all come.'

Each one of them stood still in turn to have some of the rugs, neatly rolled up, strapped to her back. They were blue and yellow and red rugs, striped, with big tassels all along the edges. N'Imah wished Laban goodbye and told him to be good and not to stand in the hot sun at midday, and then they set out. It was very pleasant along the shore, and, after an hour and a half, they came to the River Jordan which ran down into the Lake. They all splashed through it, finding the water deliciously cool to their hot hoofs, and being very careful only to step on the stones which marked the shallow part, for Jonas would have been angry if they had slipped into the water with all his rugs. Very soon they came to the village of Bethsaida.

'This is where we shall stop,' said Jonas, and he tied them up where it was shady, under some trees. There was a well close by, and first he fetched the three of them a drink of water in a round, clay bowl. Then he unpacked his rugs and spread them out, and soon his customers gathered round.

They were very queer people, and not at all like the people of Capernaum, although they were less than ten miles away. They spoke differently and they wore different clothes. They argued and even quarrelled with Jonas about the price of his rugs, but in the end they bought everything he had.

It was very hot. Jonas went away to see his friends, and Jemimah and Tirzah stood under a tree and went sound asleep standing up. They even snored a little, their heads wagging up and down even in their sleep, their ears flicking when flies settled on them. N'Imah was rather blinky, too, and she was looking lazily up the road when she saw something that made her open her eyes very wide.

Coming along the road was a little boy. He was walking very slowly and dragging his feet so that a cloud of dust flew up behind, and his grubby little fists were pushed into his eyes. Down each cheek were dirty smears where he had been crying. He came right up to the well and began to draw up some water to drink.

N'Imah felt so sorry for him that she gave a soft little bray, and he immediately turned round to look where it had come from. Under the nearest tree he saw a light-grey Donkey with big brown eyes looking at him so lovingly that he gave his eyes one last wipe with his dirty hands and went over to her. She felt so comfortable that he put his arms right round her neck and leaned up against her shaggy coat. Then he began to cry again.

'I'm so miserable,' he said. 'I can never go out and play with the other boys. We're so unhappy at home, too.'

He went on to tell N'Imah all about it. His Father was blind. He always had been blind. He couldn't play with his son or tell him stories as other fathers did, because he had never seen anything at all to tell stories about, not the house where he lived, not the Lake, or flowers or birds, not even his little boy's face.

N'Imah was so sorry about it all that she began to rub her nose up and down the boy's tunic. Just as they were getting on rather well together, they heard an angry voice shout,

'Timothy! Timothy! Where are you? Why have you left me? You've had plenty of time to get a drink.'

'Coming, Father!' cried Timothy, and away he darted.

Tap-tap, tap-tap, tap-tap. That was the blind man's stick that he used to help him feel the way. His right hand held the stick and his left hand held Timothy's, and so they shuffled sadly past together and out of sight up the road. N'Imah could hear the blind man grumbling all the time at his little boy.

'I might have fallen down or bumped into something. Why were you so long away? You can do without a drink another time, if you can't be quicker.'

N'Imah couldn't go to sleep then for thinking of Timothy. She thought about him for nearly an hour. Then she suddenly realized that there were a great many people walking past her down the road. More and more were coming every minute. They all seemed to be talking a good deal, too. Now they were collecting in groups just beyond the well. She stretched her long ears to try to find out what they were talking about, but she was too far away.

Was she dreaming? She could hardly believe her eyes. She blinked and looked again. There was no doubt about it. There was the white tunic with the silk sash, there was the face she knew and loved so well. It was Jesus. She couldn't imagine what he could be doing in Bethsaida, but there he was, walking down

the road from the village, people crowding round him and running along behind, trying to catch him up, every one trying to speak to him at once.

N'Imah stood quietly under her tree and watched. Tap-tap, tap-tap, tap-tap, came from behind her. She knew what that was. The blind man was coming back. She turned and looked over her shoulder, and there was Timothy dragging his Father along, pulling at him and shouting,

'Oh, make haste! Oh, do hurry up! We shall be too late.'

'It's no good, I tell you,' grumbled his Father. 'I've tried everything. What's the use? I never have seen and I never shall see. Oh dear! Oh dear! You'll kill me, rushing me along like this. I've a good mind to give you a bang with my stick. Just you wait till I get you home.'

'Hurry up! Hurry up!' said Timothy.

He led his Father right into the crowd, thrusting and pushing his way through it, although people did make way a little when they saw a blind man.

Straight up to Jesus, Timothy led his Father, until he stood right in front of him. Then he looked up into his face, and just said,

'Please.'

Jesus looked down into the grubby small face, all streaked with tears. Then he took the blind man's left hand in his own, and Timothy's hand in his other one, and he led them away all by themselves into the shade of the trees.

Then Jesus did a very strange thing. He spat into the palm of his hand. Next he dipped his finger into it, and carefully ran it round the blind man's eyelids.

'Can you see anything?' he asked.

'I . . . I don't know. No. Yes. I'm not very sure. There's a sort of dim light. Now there are shadows across it, tall grey shadows. Perhaps they are trees. No, they are moving about. I believe they are people! Yes, I can just see people moving about dimly.'

Again Jesus put his strong cool hands on the man's sore eyelids, and kept them there for quite a long time.

'Look again,' he said. 'What can you see now?'

The man blinked. Suddenly his eyes flew wide open.

'I can see! I can see!' he shouted. 'I can see men standing in the road! Look, there's a Donkey standing under a tree! And the sky is blue, and the sun is shining, and . . . Why! I've never seen Timothy before!'

And he stared and he stared at his little boy as if he never would stop. Then, all at once, he realized that he would never be blind any more, and, with a great shout, he threw his big stick right across the road.

'Hurrah! Hurrah!' yelled Timothy, quite forgetting himself in his excitement, and dancing up and down in the road.

'He can see! He can see! My Father is like everybody else's father!'

'Now you must both of you hurry home,' Jesus said.

'But I want to go into the village and see everything and talk to everybody.'

'No,' said Jesus. 'Go quietly home and see your own house and tell Timothy's Mother first of all.'

Timothy looked very shyly at Jesus, then he came over to him and knelt humbly down at his feet and kissed his hand, and just said, very simply,

'Thank you.'

So they went away home. Timothy and his Father, hand in hand, not because they had to but because they wanted to.

Soon the road was deserted. Jesus had gone on his way, and all the people had wandered off, some back to the village, some following him. When it grew cool, Jonas appeared.

'Home again,' he said.

Jemimah suddenly woke up and yawned.

'Eh!' she said, 'I suppose I've been dreaming. I thought I heard a great deal of noise going on here. Has anything happened?'

'Of course not,' grunted Tirzah, still half asleep. 'What do you think could happen in a village like this?'

N'Imah was tapping her hoofs with impatience.

'What do you imagine Laban will be doing?' she said. 'I hope he won't be tired of waiting for us.'

'Oh, you and your Laban!' the other two said, but they laughed at her quite kindly, and trotted along very briskly behind her.

CHAPTER TWELVE

Laban sets out on his great Adventure

AT LAST the great day came, the day they had all been waiting for. Laban was to go on his first journey. N'Imah was so excited when Jonas told them the evening before that she hardly slept a wink all night.

They were up very early. Deborah came running across the road almost as soon as she was awake. She first of all brushed Laban all over with a stiff brush, then with a soft one, so that every hair in his coat shone like silver. She polished his little hoofs with a piece of silk, and she combed his short, tufty mane with a brass comb.

'Doesn't he look lovely!' she cried, clapping her hands. 'There never was such a Donkey in all the world!'

They all stood round and admired him, and Laban stood in front of them with a smile on his face and munched away happily at the large red apple Deborah had brought him.

'A ridiculous fuss, I call it!' snorted Jemimah, rather irritably. 'Any one would think he was the only Donkey in the world! I'm sure I never brought up any of *my* children to be so fussed over.'

'Polishing his hoofs!' giggled Tirzah. 'They'll be dusty enough before he's trotted very far.'

N'Imah only wagged her head in a very wise kind of way. She did not say anything at all. She didn't quite know what was going to happen, but she felt sure that it was something very exciting and wonderful. She thought about the Prophecy.

'The Snow-white Donkey shall carry the King in his Triumph.' She wondered if she should tell Jemimah and Tirzah about it

but when she saw their scornful looks she thought that they might only laugh at her.

Now Jonas came out of his house, carrying a beautiful little halter of plaited scarlet leather, as soft as could be. It had a silver bell that hung down in front, and a scarlet tassel below that. He slipped it gently over Laban's head and it fitted him perfectly.

Where were they going? They thought it must be a long way because Jemimah and Tirzah were all packed up with parcels of dates and figs and biscuit-bread and flasks of wine, and N'Imah carried rugs for sleeping, in case all the khans were full along the road, and she had, as well, some packages of jewellery, carved beads, and little boxes of scented ointment that Jonas was going to sell on the way.

'Good-bye! Good-bye!' Deborah waved after them. 'Good-bye, Laban!' He turned and looked back at her lovingly out of his shining dark-blue eyes, before he turned the last corner of the main street, going out of the town.

Right round the side of the Lake they went, and N'Imah remembered how she had come that way when she was a baby Donkey, not nearly as big or as strong as Laban was now.

'Perhaps we are going to Nazareth,' she said to Laban, 'to the Little House where your Grandmother lived.'

But they did not turn aside. Straight on they went, all along the river valley. It was very pleasant there, with palm trees and grass and the silver river itself. They stopped many times and Jonas met many friends, and so two weeks went by before they realized.

'How far are you travelling, Jonas?' his friends called out to him.

'I'm going to the Temple for the Great Feast, of course,' Jonas answered them, but he had a strange little smile on his face, as if he had a secret that he wasn't going to tell.

'We're going to Jerusalem!' said Jemimah, in a pleased voice.

'Just fancy! We're going to Jerusalem,' echoed Tirzah.

She turned rather condescendingly to Laban.

'That will be something new for you,' she said.

Laban only looked at her out of his big solemn eyes. He did not make any answer.

'Is it a big place?' N'Imah asked, innocently. 'Bigger than Capernaum?'

Jemimah and Tirzah stared at her for a minute, then they burst out laughing rather rudely at her ignorance.

Laban trotted all the way behind them, and Jonas was very careful not to let him get too tired. He even brushed his coat and bathed his hoofs in cold water every night, when they stopped at a wayside khan or camped out under the palm trees. Laban had special things to eat, too, armfuls of luscious young grass, for it was early spring, and barley and soaked beans.

About the third week they came to the loveliest place they had ever seen. Its name was Jericho. It was just like summer there.

It was warm all the year round, and even in winter the people went about in thin silks or shining white linen. There were groves of palm trees waving gently in the summery breeze, and little rivulets of water on all sides, and great gardens of roses and balsam, all scenting the air right out as far as the sea. Why, the very name Jericho meant 'The Scented Place'! There were palaces with dazzling white walls, a place for games and races, and wonderful gardens all laid out with different kinds of fruit and flowers. It was a fairy-land of a place. People of every kind thronged the streets, travellers and rich merchants, traders from all lands, soldiers and courtiers and even robbers. They saw camels and Arab horses and mules and Donkeys, some carrying riders and some drawing waggons.

Laban opened his eyes very wide and pushed in close to N'Imah, because every one began to stare at the pure white Donkey with the scarlet harness.

'Hey, Jonas!' a big man with a black beard shouted after them, 'I'll give you a bag of silver for the white colt.'

Jonas shook his head, smiling.

'He's not for sale.'

'Come now, I'll give you a fine Arab Horse for him. Whoever heard before of a Donkey being exchanged for a horse?'

'He's not for sale,' said Jonas, and again he smiled that strange, secret smile.

They moved on, out of Jericho, leaving the sweet scents of the rose gardens and all the exciting crowds of people behind.

'Oh, dear!' sighed Jemimah, who really was getting rather old and crotchety. 'I thought we were going to stay there for a time. I saw a good many old friends I should like to have had a chat with, Donkeys I used to know when I was in Jerusalem before.'

The road went uphill now, and was rather stony, and they left the shining river behind. All round them were queer, twisted trees with grey trunks, all gnarled and knotted so that they looked like ugly old men. They were just coming into leaf, and even their leaves were silvery-grey and made little whispering noises when they rubbed against each other.

'Brrrrr!' said young Laban, looking rather frightened and putting his long ears back.

'Silly!' Tirzah laughed at him. 'They're only olive trees.'

When they had climed right up to the top of the steep hill, they came to a cross-roads, and there was a tiny village, really only a cluster of little white houses.

'We can't be going to stay here!' said Jemimah.

But they were. Out of the first house came two men. They drew Jonas to one side and they all began to whisper together.

'He will send when he is ready,' said one, softly.

'They will be quite safe here until then,' murmured the other.

'When?' asked Jonas.

'In about three days,' the first man answered. 'But you must not speak of it to a single soul. There is danger.'

What could the mystery be? Jemimah and Tirzah stretched out their ears as far as they could, to listen, but N'Imah smiled to herself. She felt more and more sure that the great adventure of Laban's small life was coming very near.

So Jonas handed N'Imah and Laban over to the two strangers.

'You must wait here,' he said to them, very kindly. 'I and the other two must go on. We have some trading to do before we go into Jerusalem, but I shall see you again.'

They felt a little forlorn and frightened when they saw the grey backs of Jemimah and Tirzah trotting away from them with Jonas.

'Well I never!' they heard Jemimah's voice coming back through the trees. 'What can the great mystery be?'

They were left tied up outside the house. N'Imah and her snow-white son. It was warm, spring weather and they had nothing to do. They could hear people talking inside. They sounded very excited, very thrilled about something, and yet they always spoke in whispers, as if they were afraid of being heard. Laban was brushed again and again, and given delicious things to eat, fresh barley brought from Jericho especially for him. Even his little red halter was polished. His coat was more shining than ever, his eyes brighter, and his velvety nose twitched with excitement.

It was about noon on the third day. They looked down the road and they saw, climbing up towards them, two men in white tunics and striped coats of brown and yellow. Nearer they came, and nearer. Now N'Imah could see that one of them was quite young, very boyish-looking, in fact, with curly hair. The other was older, with a little grey in his thick hair and in his beard.

They paused at the cross-roads.

'This is the place, Peter,' said the younger of the two.

'And there is the white colt, John,' answered the other. 'How beautiful he looks in the sunlight!'

N'Imah's heart beat very fast. It had come then. This must be the great moment when her son was to fulfil the Prophecy.

The men moved quietly over to Laban and began to untie him. He seemed to know that he had to go, for he rubbed his head against them.

'What are you doing?' said a voice, suddenly, and out of the house came the people who lived there. 'Why are you loosing the colt?'

Peter and John stood quite still for a minute, then John said, very quietly,

'The Lord hath need of him.'

There was silence. You could almost hear N'Imah's heart thumping. Then the men from the house bowed their heads and said nothing at all.

Peter and John went away, and between them trotted Laban, his head well up, the plume on the end of his tail swishing with pride. N'Imah watched him go, and she, too, felt proud. To-day, this very day, Laban would become famous. She stood quite still and watched him out of sight.

Down the hill went Laban. He knew what was going to happen. He was going to meet the King.

Now people were coming up towards him. Now a little group of them began to call out to Peter and John. Now more and more people were coming in sight.

'Stand still,' whispered John, in his ear.

The crowd parted, and out of its midst stepped the King. He only wore a simple white tunic but Laban knew at once, that he was the King. He looked up into his face, and his knees trembled, because he was very young and this was such a very great occasion. He looked up into the kindest eyes he had ever

seen, and his knees stopped trembling. He knew him. Yes, of course he knew him. This was Jesus, about whom his mother, N'Imah, had told him such wonderful stories.

Then some of the people began to take off their gay striped coats and cloaks, and they laid them on Laban's strong little back because he hadn't a saddle. Across his own dazzling white coat were coats of orange and yellow stripes, of emerald green and scarlet and nut brown. Then Jesus drew near, and all his friends knelt down and held out their arms to make steps for

him to mount, and, in a second, he was safely seated on Laban's back.

Away they went. The people all laughed and shouted with joy. The road was rocky, but they didn't mind. On the left was a steep slope down into the valley, and on the right was the upwards slope of the Mount of Olives. Out of all the cracks in the rocks sprang fig-trees, for this was called the Little Country of Figs.

How merrily they went along! How they cheered! More and more people came running from every direction and joined in. Soon you could not even see the end of the crowd. Over a ridge they went, and there lay Jerusalem before them, all gold and white, all towers and domes and palaces and castles.

Now the children were running out, such jolly, rosy-cheeked, brown-legged children, laughing and cheering louder than any one. Out of the houses they came tumbling. Faces smiled out of every window, doors burst open, feet came clattering down steps and stairs. You would not think there could be so many children in all the world as came running out to see Jesus the King go riding by on Laban's back.

Out came young Bartholomew, the goldsmith's son. He was so excited that he seized Laban's red halter and skipped along with it in his hand. His sister, Anna, was nursing the baby, but out she ran, too, with him in her arms, and even the baby clapped his fat little hands together with delight. Out came Thomas and Paul and Dorcas and Barnabas.

'Let's make a path for the King!' shouted Seth, the innkeeper's son.

'Yes! A path, a path for the King!' shouted all of them.

They ran about wildly and gathered branches from the trees and leaves from their gardens, and threw them down on the road under Laban's feet. He tossed his head with joy, and picked up his polished hoofs as high as he possibly could and fairly pranced into Jersualem.

'Hosanna!' shouted the children.

'Hosanna!'

'Hosanna in the Highest!' they echoed each other.

It echoed along the streets and right up into the air, so that even the sky and the earth and the trees and the houses all seemed to be shouting 'Hosanna!' together, and above all the singing and the shouting and the laughing you could hear quite clearly, if you listened carefully, Laban's little silver bell tinkling.

So they went right into Jerusalem, right up to the outside walls of the Temple, and the sun shone on all of them, and they waved their palm branches, and sang their songs, and little Seth even turned cart-wheels all the way, and the King's hand rested very kindly and gently on Laban's white neck.

CHAPTER THIRTEEN

In which Laban weeps for sadness

LABAN STOOD OUTSIDE the house and felt very lonely. There he was, back in the Little Village of Fig Trees, tied up just where he had been before he went on his great Adventure. He almost thought it was all a dream; but then he remembered how Peter and John had brought him back and tied him up there. N'Imah had gone. Jonas had been and fetched her away, so that Laban was all alone.

He stood very still and thought about what had happened. He went carefully over the whole story, beginning right back at the Angel his Mother had told him about, the Angel who had come straight out of the sky, right down to the very field where his Grandmother, Trottemenu, had been standing. Everything had come true. He, Laban, really had gone trotting into Jerusalem itself, palm branches under his hoofs, his white mane tossing in the sunlight, and the King seated on his back! What fun it had all been! He remembered the gay, striped cloaks they had thrown across him, the singing and the shouting and the laughter, the tinkling of his silver bell, and little Seth letting go of the scarlet halter to turn cart-wheels all along the street. Then Jesus had left them and gone quietly into the Temple, and Peter and John had brought Laban back, and that was all.

He wrinkled up his forehead, very puzzled. Somehow, he had not expected it to end like that, so suddenly. He wanted N'Imah. He wanted to tell her all about it and to ask her why it was all over so quickly, and what the King was doing now, but he didn't even know where N'Imah had gone. At that moment he would have been glad of Jemimah to talk to, even if she laughed at him. His new Owners inside the house were quite kind to him, but he just could not make them understand how lonely and puzzled he felt.

It was his second night there. It was getting dark. He huddled up close to the house wall and stared at the little square of lantern light that came through the window. All round him the trees were whispering together and making strange noises, and under them and between them was a great pool of blackness. He thought he could hear footsteps coming up the road; he thought he could see, just dimly, something white. Then out of the shadows stepped Peter and John.

'They're coming to fetch me again!' thought Laban. 'The King needs me again!'

He gave a soft little bray of delight; but Peter and John did not seem to see him or hear him. They went silently past and knocked in a strange, hurried way at the door.

'Rat-tat-a-tat!' then three slow knocks, almost as if it were a signal.

Instantly, the Owners came out. They all stood in the doorway and whispered together in the dark.

'Where is he now?' some one asked.

'At Bethany, just over a mile away,' Peter answered in a low voice.

'Is it safe?'

'He is with his friends.'

'All the same, there is danger.'

'He goes to Jerusalem every day and comes back to Bethany every night,' said John. 'His enemies would hardly follow him there.'

'It is dangerous. We don't know where they would lie in wait for him.'

'What do you think they would do to him?'

'They would kill him if they could.'

Laban stood there in the dark and shivered. He knew that they were talking about the King—*his* King, for hadn't he carried him on his back into Jerusalem? Laban was frightened now. He had no one to talk to, no one to ask, and Jesus the King was in some terrible danger.

Soon the moon rose, and the shadowy trees were not quite so frightening then. The house was silent, and Laban stood against the house wall, a little silvery-white Donkey with silver hoofs in the moonlight, thinking and thinking how he could save the King.

But the days went by and nothing happened. One day, two days, three days passed. Sometimes the house was quite empty and Laban's Owners were away for hours at a time. Sometimes they were at home, and then they talked and talked in whispers, as if they were making plans for something very important and very secret. Sometimes visitors came, late at night, wrapped in dark cloaks, and joined in the talks.

Laban had been there over a week. It was Thursday evening and he stood outside in the moonlight. He was not cold, for his white furry coat was thick, but he felt restless. The world looked very strange at that time of night; the house walls glittered like icing, the olive leaves shivered until they showed all white underneath, and the twisty trunks were turned to silver. It was very quiet. One by one the voices inside the house died out. Now he could hear the sleeping mats being pulled out onto the floor. Now the lantern was taken from the wall and put low down, so that it threw no light out of the window. Silence—nothing but silence. It was very late, nearly midnight. Gradually a shadow crept across the house wall as the moon moved across the sky, and Laban stood in the shadow and wondered, a little sadly, if anything exciting would ever happen to him again.

His ears jerked up. His mane prickled all along its length. Somewhere, down in the olive wood, some one was moving. Some one was pushing up through the trees, running. Whoever it was, they were not very sure of themselves, for they were stumbling. They were out of breath, too. Laban could hear him now, almost sobbing for breath. Nearly midnight, and some one was running and stumbling up towards the silent house.

Some one came out of the woods, out of the shadows and into the moonlight.

Why, it was only a boy, after all! Just a boy of about sixteen.

But his eyes were staring with fear, glittering, and his face was white with terror. Across his forehead was a great purple bruise.

He rushed up to the closed door and began to beat on it with his clenched fists as if he were mad.

'Let me in!' he cried. 'Let me in!'

Bang! Bang! Bang! his hands went, on the heavy door. Inside the house there was whispering.

'Don't open the door,' some one said, quite clearly. 'It's a trap.'

'But suppose it's a message for us?'

'Not at this time of night. Besides, if it were a friend he would give the signal knock.'

'Let me in! Open the door and let me in!' shouted the boy, frantically.

'Who is it?'

'Mark.[1] It's Mark, from Jerusalem.'

'Let him in,' said a voice from inside. 'Something terrible must have happened.'

Very cautiously they opened the door, and one of them held the lantern up to Mark's face.

'He's injured!' some one cried. 'Look at his head!'

Mark stood in the doorway and looked at them, his eyes wide open. Then he swayed slightly, and fell in a heap on the floor.

'Get some water!'

'No, get wine. Force some between his lips.'

'There is that green spice-ointment for his head.'

They ran about, fetching everything they could think of, and soon Mark was lying on a couch watching them. They gave him wine and water to drink, and tied up his head with ointment and a white linen bandage. Then they began to ask him what had happened. Mark shuddered.

'Our King—' he began, 'Jesus, our King—'

'Where is he? What has happened? Is he safe?'

'He has been captured. A band of soldiers with swords and great sticks took him prisoner. They have taken him to the Palace of Annas.'

[1] Mark's name was really John Mark, and he was always called John at home, but as there is another John in this story, he is called by his second name.

The men in the room jumped up and walked about.

'What are we to do?' they said. 'Will the others try to rescue him? What can we do against armed soldiers?'

Then they turned again to Mark and began to question him, all speaking at once. How did he know all this? Had he seen it for himself? How did he get the bruise on his head? Where had he been? Mark did not know which question to answer first.

'Let him begin at the beginning,' then said one. 'Let him tell us the whole story. Come along, Mark. There is nothing to be afraid of here.'

So Mark sat up on the couch, looking almost as white as his bandages.

'You know my Father's house?' he began. 'Right in the City, that big house where the Damascus Road begins?'

They nodded.

'Well, I knew something exciting was going to happen days ago. My Mother had all the house specially cleaned, and my Father seemed so excited, as if something splendid were going to happen. When I asked them, they only said that I wasn't old enough to know yet, but afterwards they would tell me. Well, this afternoon I hadn't anything to do and I was thinking about the Great Feast. I thought I'd like to go upstairs and look out of the top window at all the crowds coming into the town. You know, we have quite a big room up there, and we only use it for very special parties. It used to be a flat roof, and then we had it covered in. Anyway, I went up there and opened the door and walked in.'

'Go on!' said his listeners, as he paused. 'What happened next?'

'Well, it was rather queer. There was a table all set for supper in the middle of the room, and couches and rugs all round it. There was a flagon of red wine on the table, and a pile of dry wafer-bread, and bunches of herbs and dates and raisins. I was standing staring, because I hadn't known we were going to have visitors. Suddenly, I heard a sound behind me, and there was Mother. She was looking quite worried and cross. "Oh Mark!" she said, "you shouldn't be up here at all. Go away at once. And you mustn't tell any one you've been here." She pushed me out of the door and shut it behind me.'

'What did you do then?'

'I couldn't think of anything to do. I stood out in the street for some time, watching the crowds. Then I wandered into our courtyard. There was Nathan, our servant, filling all the water-pots. He's rather a cross old man, always grumbling. "Are we having visitors, Nathan?" I asked. But he wouldn't answer, only grunted. Then he did something that I've never seen him do before. He took our biggest water-pot, full of water, and hoisted it up on his shoulder. "Hi, Nathan," I said, 'you know one of the maids always does that. Why don't you call Martha or Rachel?" And do you know what he said? He turned right round and just said, "You mind your own business, Master Mark." Then he marched out of the yard with the water-pot on his shoulder and went up the street with it. I can tell you I was astonished.'

Mark paused to take a sip of water, then he went on again.

'Of course, I hung about after that. I knew something was going to happen. There's a little room opposite the upstairs one, so I went and hid in that and kept the door open a crack. I could see into the courtyard, too, through the window. I suppose it was about an hour before Nathan came back, and he was still carrying that great pitcher. He hadn't been in the courtyard a minute before Peter and John came in. Of course, I knew them by sight. My Father came out from down below and spoke to them, and then they came up the outside staircase and went into the room opposite. I dared not look out, because I was afraid my Father might be with them. I could hear them moving about inside the room. It sounded as if they were getting things ready. All the while I was puzzling and puzzling over that water-pot. Then I thought that the supper was perhaps a great secret, and the jug of water was a sort of secret signal so that Peter and John would know which house to come to.

'Well, when they'd finished, they went away. I was determined to stay and see who the guests were going to be. I seemed to have been up there for hours. I wanted to sneeze, because it was dusty. Then I was hungry, and I hadn't had my supper, so I crept down again and took some bread from the kitchen while Martha was outside talking. It grew dark, and then the moon came up and made it light again. Hours and hours seemed to go by. No one seemed to miss me, no one came to look for me. I thought I'd give it up, and then, all at once, I heard a lot of people talking down below.'

His hearers sat absorbed, their chins in their hands. Mark went on:

'I couldn't escape then, for they were all coming up the outside staircase. I could hear their sandals rubbing, and some of them were whispering. I stood against the crack of the door, and they passed so close to me that I could have touched them. I knew Peter and John, of course. Then there was Judas, that big man with a red beard. Then—and then—'

Mark's voice suddenly grew shrill with excitement. He could hardly speak.

'Then—what do you think? There was Jesus himself! I only had to put my hand out to feel his sleeve! I nearly rushed out and asked if I could go in to the supper with them. I was just getting up courage to do it, when they all went into the big room and shut the door.

'I was so disappointed, I can tell you. I nearly cried. I could hear them talking in there, and there I was outside, covered with dust and with nowhere to go. I thought I might as well creep down to the kitchen again, and see if Martha knew anything about the supper party. Sometimes, when she's not too busy, she'll talk to me. I was just half-way down the staircase into the courtyard, when some one began to come up. I tried to go back, but it was too late. There stood my Father. He looked terribly angry. "Mark," he said, "what are you doing up here?" "I wanted to see who was going to the supper upstairs, Father," I answered. He didn't say anything for a minute, then he said, quite kindly, "Well, my boy, you have been very near to great things to-night. One day you will understand, but now they must be for those who are older and wiser than you. Go off to bed now, and give no trouble to-night."

'Well, of course, I had to go after that. My bedroom was under the big room, though, and I lay in bed and listened to the murmur of voices. I couldn't make out what they said. Once I thought I heard some one get up from the table and go downstairs and across the courtyard. At last I heard them begin to move, then I heard them singing. I could hear the words quite plainly:

"O praise the Lord all ye nations,
Praise him all ye people."

Then they all began to put on their sandals that they had left just inside the door, and I heard them go downstairs.'

Mark paused here, and lay back on the couch. He looked paler and paler, yet his hearers were sure that the most important part of the story was still to come, and they were impatient for him to continue. At last, with an effort, Mark sat up, but he looked round him all the time as if he were nearly mad with fear.

'Tell us the rest,' they begged him, and Mark pulled himself together and went on:

'I suppose I must have gone to sleep after that. I don't remember anything until I jumped up in bed with my heart thumping like a drum. I could hear soldiers down below. I heard the rattle of armour and the clink of swords, and rough voices and swearing. I heard their heavy feet go up the staircase and into the top room. I was terribly frightened. My throat seemed to dry up, so that I couldn't cry out for help. I heard them stamping about up above, then one of them called out, "They've escaped! After them, fellows, and hound them down!"

'They growled like a pack of dogs, as, pushing each other and grumbling and swearing, they went off. I peeped out of the window and saw that they'd left torches and lanterns on poles in the courtyard.

'I don't know now why I did it. I think I meant to warn Jesus. I picked up my linen wrap from the side of my bed, and huddled it round me, and followed them. I was shivering with cold and—I don't mind telling you—fright. I hadn't even time to put on my sandals.

'I followed them right out of the North Gate, down into the Black Valley. I'd never been there alone before. It was terrible.

The Kidron River was tearing along, very nearly in flood, and dark and muddy, and it was so black in there among the trees that you couldn't even see the soldiers, except where the lantern made a red glow here and there. You could hear the clink of their armour, though.

'First we turned left, then we turned right. Then we came to a high wall, and they all stopped. Suddenly I realized where we were. It was the Garden of Gethsemane. There was a high wall all round, and inside there were shrubberies of flowering trees. You know the place, don't you? There's a kind of building at the entrance with an old press for squeezing out oil. That's where we stopped. The soldiers stuck the lantern-poles in the ground. I kept in the shadow, close to the wall.

'Then, all at once, I saw something that gave me an awful shock. Judas was talking to them! Judas, who'd been at the supper in our house!'

'So it was Judas!' said one of the listening men. 'The traitor! We'll kill him for this!'

They were wild with fury. They could hardly listen to Mark's quiet voice.

'I edged up close,' he went on, 'and heard him say, "Is the arrangement quite clear? I'll go straight up and kiss him as the signal. Then you can close up behind me and take him." I'm sure now that it was Judas who went downstairs while I was lying in bed. He went to fetch the soldiers.

'I tried to shout. I tried to shout a warning, but my voice stuck in my throat. Then it all seemed to happen at once. I don't quite know what did happen. The soldiers all rushed forward with the lanterns. I could hear people trampling through the trees in every direction. Then I heard them coming back. They were marching back. And they had Jesus in the midst of them, his hands lashed together with ropes. And Judas stood and watched, smiling. All at once, I think I went mad. I rushed at him, yelling and hitting out with my fists. Then a soldier came for me. He hurled himself on me, and knocked me down and fell on top of me. I felt his face, where he hadn't shaved, rough on mine, and I felt his hot breath. I wriggled from under him and dashed off. I could hear his feet pounding after me. I turned to look over my shoulder, and crashed my head against a tree. his hands came out; he caught my linen wrap and clutched at it. I just managed to let it go. I slid out of it and went on running, I don't know where.

'I don't know when I came to my senses. I suddenly felt sick and my teeth were chattering. I crept home, down the back way. I crept into the house. I couldn't find my Mother or my Father. I could hear Martha, down in the courtyard, telling Nathan that they had all gone to the Palace of Annas. In my room I found my other tunic and a coat and my sandals, and put them on, then I came to look for you.'

'You did well, Mark,' one of them said. 'You have been very brave.'

'But what are we going to do?'

'What can we do? I don't know. But at least we can get all his friends together and go into the City. Where are Peter and John?'

'They went with him, I think.'

'Well, now, Mark, you lie back and rest for a while, and we will make plans. As soon as it is daylight we will all go into Jerusalem and find out what has happened.'

Everything was silent now. Laban, leaning up against the outside wall, thought that Mark must be sleeping. He wished it were daylight. He wished he were in Jerusalem. He wished he could untie himself and go off without waiting for any one else. Never, never had a night seemed so long.

At last it was over. It grew dark as the moon set, then it grew grey, then faint streaks of daylight began to appear. The house door opened. The young men of the house half led, half carried Mark. He looked dreadfully ill, but as if he were glad to be going back. Laban pressed up as close as his rope would let him. Would they take him? He couldn't, he couldn't be left behind!'

'Please!' his eyes said. 'Please!'

'Oh dear,' one of them said, 'I'd forgotten the white colt. What shall we do with him?'

'We'd better take him,' said the other. 'We don't know when we shall be back.'

Laban nearly went rushing off down the hill as soon as they untied him, he was so anxious to be there.

Mark walked very slowly. His head hurt him.

'We can't let you ride the colt,' said one of his friends, 'because, of course, it belongs to our King, but I don't see why you shouldn't lean on him.'

So they went down the stony hill, full of fears and unhappiness, Mark leaning against Laban's silky back, every stone in the road jarring his bruised head.

Right down into the City they went, straight to Mark's home. They left Laban outside, and they all disappeared into the house. Soon the young men came out; but Mark they had left behind with his Mother. They went away up the street, and they never even looked at Laban.

There he stood all day. No one came to tell him what was happening. No one spoke to him. Once Nathan came out and threw him some dried grass, but he wouldn't eat it. In the afternoon the sun went in and the sky grew dark, but still Laban stood there, alone and forgotten. It began to draw towards evening. People began to come along the road in twos and threes. Did Laban imagine it, or did they all look rather sad and frightened? No one seemed to speak. No one smiled. A great cold fear suddenly clutched Laban's heart. If only he knew. If only he could find out the truth. He looked at people pleadingly, but they only glanced at him and turned away. They only saw a solitary little white Donkey, tied up against a house wall.

Then he saw a familiar form, ambling down the road. He couldn't be mistaken. He knew that dusty grey coat, that grumpy walk. He recognized her even before he heard her grumbling away to herself.

'Jemimah!' he called out. 'Oh, Jemimah! Please stay and talk to me for a minute.'

'Well, only for a minute,' she said. 'My Owner's just behind. At least, my owner for a few days. He's only borrowed me to get all his work done before the Great Feast. Tirzah and your Mother are waiting for me outside the City, and I shall be joining them again in a day or two.'

'Oh Jemimah!' said Laban, trembling all over, 'have you heard any news in the City? Any news about Jesus the King?'

Jemimah turned her head and looked at Laban very pityingly.

'Haven't you heard?' she said. 'You will never see your King any more. The King is dead. They took him out on to a hill just outside the City early this morning, and there they killed him. They made a big cross out of an oak tree, and they nailed him on it, and he died.'

Laban did not hear or see Jemimah go. He did not even notice when her Owner came along, or what else Jemimah may have said. He stood against the wall, his head hanging down, and the great, heavy tears rolled down his face, making deep furrows in his furry cheeks.

CHAPTER FOURTEEN

In which Laban becomes famous for evermore

ALL THAT NIGHT and all the next day Laban stood there. They tempted him with fresh grass, with beans, even with barley, but he just turned his face away from them all. Mark brought him an earthenware bowl full of clear, cool water, but he would not drink. His friends from the Village of Figs came and stroked him and spoke gently to him, but he just gazed sadly at them out of his big dark-blue eyes, then turned away again, towards the wall.

'He will die,' Mark said, nearly crying himself. 'He will die of hunger.'

They tried everything. They searched the town for fresh fruit and vegetables for him, they held them to his mouth, they petted him and coaxed him, but all in vain. Laban did not want to live. His heart was broken. He had given all his love and all his loyalty to his King, and now his King was dead and he would never see him again. So he turned his face to the wall and refused to speak to any one. His coat lost its silkiness and was harsh and ruffled, his velvety nose felt hot and dry.

By Sunday he was so weak that he had to lean against the wall to keep up on his hoofs. It was such a gentle spring day, too, with little puffy clouds like swansdown floating across the deep blue of the sky, and the white walls of the houses shining as if they had just been washed. Mark's Mother had a row of plants on a windowsill, and they had all suddenly burst out into clusters of scarlet flowers. It was a day to be happy in, but Laban stood there and felt that he would never be happy any more.

He hardly noticed Mark's Mother when she came out of the

house in the middle of the morning and passed quite close to him, and even looked pityingly at him. It was not very long, either, before she was back again. She came hurrying up the street, almost running, so that the white veil she wore over her hair streamed out behind her. She came into the courtyard like that, and, long before she reached the house door, she began to call out,

'Mark! Mark! Where are you?'

She called so loudly and in such an excited voice that Mark's Father came out.

'Mary!' he said, in surprise. 'What can have happened? They will hear you right up the street!'

And she laughed! She actually laughed. Mark came hurrying out at that moment.

'Oh Mother!' he said, as astonished as his Father was. 'What can be the matter?'

'Such wonderful news!' she cried. 'I can hardly get my breath to tell you! I ran nearly all the way home.'

'Do calm yourself then,' said her husband. 'People will wonder whatever you have been doing.'

'But such news!' she said. 'Such wonderful news! We shall see the King again!'

Mark stared at her. His Mother was usually so calm and quiet. He never remembered seeing her like this before. Her brown eyes, generally so thoughtful, were shining with excitement, and her smooth brown hair, which he never remembered seeing in the least untidy, was actually all ruffled up where her veil and the wind had tugged at it.

She laughed when she saw Mark staring at her, looking so puzzled, and slid one arm round him.

'It's quite true,' she said. 'I thought I would go and see my cousin Ruth this morning, to see if she had any fresh news. She always knows the latest news about everything. As soon as I came within sight of the house, I knew that something had happened. All her neighbours were there, running in and out of the front door, all talking at once. The kitchen was absolutely full of women, and there sat Ruth in the middle of them as if she hadn't any housework to do at all. As soon as she saw me she jumped up and called out, "Oh, I'm so glad you've come, Cousin Mary! Have you heard?" "Heard what?" I said. "I don't know what you're talking about." '

'Oh, Mother!' said Mark, impatiently, 'do tell us what's happened, and never mind Cousin Ruth and her neighbours!'

'I'll tell my story in my own way,' said his Mother, teasing him.

'Well, they all began to try to tell me at once, till Ruth said, "No, I'll tell her. I heard the story first." Well, Ruth has a great many friends outside the town, and some of them came up to Jerusalem with Jesus and stayed with him right up to the end.'

Mark's eyes suddenly opened very wide and he fixed them on his Mother's face, waiting.

'One of them, Mary Magdalene, Ruth said, found out where they had laid him after they had taken him down from the Cross. It was in a lovely little garden, outside the City, in a cave between two big black cypress trees. Now she is very clever at making scented ointments and spice-sachets out of plants and flower-petals, and she thought she would take some secretly to the cave, because she wanted it to be a kind of very special last gift to the King, whom she would never see again. She couldn't go yesterday, because it was the Sabbath, so she had to wait until this morning. She thought that if she went very early, before it was light, no one would see her. So she crept out of the house and out through the Town Gate, and made her way to the garden.'

'Oh, go on!' burst out Mark, trembling with eagerness. 'Do go on, Mother!'

'It was so early that it was shadowy in there, and the grass was long and very wet with dew, and Mary said that she could smell hyacinths in the grass. Then all at once she remembered a terrible thing. She couldn't imagine how she could have forgotten it. The mouth of the cave was blocked with an enormous stone. It would have taken six men to roll it away. She nearly turned back, then, but she was so near that she thought she would at least go and look.

'She couldn't see the stone. She thought that the shadow of

the cypresses was so black over it. Then she realized that it was moved to one side. The cave stood open.'

'Yes! Yes! And then!' said Mark, breathlessly.

'Just at that moment, she heard somebody coming. She could hear them swishing through the wet grass and brushing against the bushes. It was a dreadful moment. She did not want the soldiers to find her there. She did not make a sound, hardly breathed as she slid into the shadow of one of the cypresses. She could see a glimmer of colour, blue-grey and purple, and then she realized that it was the other women coming on the same errand as herself, secretly.

'They stood there for a little while, half-afraid, then they tiptoed up to the cave and looked in.

'It was dark. It was dark and rocky and full of shadows. But, as they looked, there seemed to be a faint light, in one corner, on their right. It grew and grew, like a misty gold cloud, and in the middle of the cloud were white wings. Brighter and brighter it shone, until suddenly they were looking at a young man sitting there. His face gave out a golden light, his hair streamed back like flames, and he wore a tunic that was white and yet more dazzling than white, as if it were woven out of clouds.

'Ruth was not quite sure what happened next. Mary could hardly tell the story clearly, it was all so strange, but the Angel sitting there told them that they would see the King again, that he was not dead.'

'Oh Mother!' breathed Mark. 'If only we could have been there!'

'Wait, Mark!' said his Mother. 'That is not the end. Mary and the others had only one thought. They must tell Peter and John. They turned round and all began to run. They went stumbling through the grass in their hurry, and their dresses were all soaked with dew and clung to them as they ran. If any one had seen them then they would surely have stopped them.'

'What did Peter and John do?'

'They went running off, as hard as they could go. Of course, John got there first.'

Mark laughed. 'Poor old Peter! But John isn't really so very much older than I am.'

'But then, John got suddenly frightened, and he daredn't look inside. Peter dashed in before him.'

'And did they see the Angel?'

'No, they didn't.'

His Mother's bright face clouded over for a minute, and she looked puzzled.

'It was quite dim again, in there. But something white was lying on the ground. Peter stooped down to look. It was the white linen cloths that had been wrapped round Jesus. They didn't know what to think. They didn't know whether to believe Mary's story about an Angel or not. She met them, just coming away again, and they would hardly stop to talk to her. They wanted to hurry back to see what their friends thought of it all.

'It was light now. She could see dark marks in the wet grass where Peter and John had run through it. She could see the hyacinths, pale blue and white, like candles, and there was a bush covered with flowers like tiny white stars. A blackbird began to whistle, and there was a lovely golden light everywhere. There were even little rainbows hanging in the drops of water on the grass-blades. But there wasn't any Angel. The cave was empty, except for that strange little heap of white linen. Mary stood gazing in so long, that she hardly knew what she did see. Once she thought that there were two faintly golden patches, but the tears blurred her eyes, and when she had wiped them away, there was nothing there. The cave was empty, and Peter and John hadn't believed her story.

'She was just turning away. She stopped dead. There was some one standing behind her. She was frightened. It might be a soldier. Or it might be the gardener, who would be angry with her for being there. She looked up, and there, all white and shining, in a haze of golden light, was the King himself.'

There was silence. Then Mark drew a long breath and looked expectantly at his Father. Surely his Father was going to say something. He had been silent all through the story.

Then, 'I don't believe it!' he said.

'Father!' Mark cried.

'I don't believe a word of it. It's a pack of idle tales.'

'But Father!'

'The women made it all up. Or else they dreamed it.'

Mark felt as if the whole house were going to fall down on top of him. His lips quivered. He looked at his Mother. She didn't say a word, only hurried into the house.

Laban lifted his head. It couldn't be true! Lovely things like that didn't happen any more. But suppose it were true? Why, he felt a little stronger just for thinking about it! He absentmindedly stretched out his neck and took a little mouthful of dried grass, although it tasted like sawdust on his tongue. All the same, he began to look up when people passed through the courtyard now, because he hoped that some one else would come and say more about the story.

Something was certainly going to happen in the house. Martha and Rachel kept looking out of the window, and Nathan went in and out very busily. Laban was sure that visitors were coming. Mark, too, behaved very oddly, sulky at one minute and then almost cheerful the next.

Towards evening people did begin to come. They came in ones and twos, rather quietly and secretly. They all seemed to greet Mark's Father with the whispered words, 'Have you heard? Have you heard?'

'Yes, and I don't believe it,' he answered, crossly. 'What's more, I believe it's a trap. They want to get us all together, talking about it, and then they'll take us all prisoner. If you take my advice, you'll come inside the house quickly and lock all the doors.'

At this the visitors began to look very alarmed.

'Are we going to meet in the top room again?' Peter asked.

'Yes, the same room. Supper will be ready later on. But do come inside now.'

Stealthily they went in, almost as if they were afraid that the soldiers were hiding in the courtyard to leap out on them. Soon they were all inside, and every door was shut tight and locked and barred from within.

It was very quiet outside, so quiet that Laban could hear them talking if he listened, although he could not make out the words. Once he heard Mark's Father talk to old Nathan downstairs.

'Don't tell me such silly tales, Nathan,' he said, angrily. 'Get on with your work. And you, Martha. No one believes such nonsense.'

Suddenly, Mark's voice rang out, clear and loud and defiant,

'I do, Father!'

Surely they had all been inside the house a very long time. It seemed very late to Laban. The street outside was deserted, not a footstep rang on the pavement. All at once it seemed to him that they were very quiet up there. Almost as if something had happened. He cocked up his long ears, the first time for days. Nothing. What could they be doing.

It was moonlight now, past the full moon, but quite light. How queer the shadows looked! Dark-blue shapes on white walls. Even his own shadow looked queer, all long ears and long legs. Surely that door had been closed, and now it stood wide open?

He had the strangest feeling, as if something were going to happen to him. He stood perfectly still, waiting. Then he heard it.

'Laban!'

The voice spoke so softly that he wondered if it was only inside his own head.

'Laban!'

It seemed to come from above. He looked up, his face white in the moonlight, his eyes shining, dark-blue pools.

Someone stood at the window above. Someone in a shining white robe. Someone was smiling down at him. It was Jesus, his King.

'Laban, My faithful little Friend,' he said, and stretched out his hands lovingly towards the little white Donkey. 'Because you have been so faithful to me, you shall be known from now onwards, for ever and ever, as Laban the Kingbearer.'